VESTIGES OF A JOURNEY

Sabas Whittaker

Copyright © 2000 by Sabas Whittaker.

ISBN #:   Softcover   0-7388-3600-1

All rights reserved. No part of this book may be reproduced or transmitted in any form or by any means, electronic or mechanical, including photocopying, recording, or by any information storage and retrieval system, without permission in writing from the copyright owner.

This book was printed in the United States of America.

To order additional copies of this book, contact:
Xlibris Corporation
1-888-7-XLIBRIS
www.Xlibris.com
Orders@Xlibris.com

CONTENTS

Preface 13
Acknowledgments 15
Autobiography 17
My Grandma 19
Happy Mother's Day 21
Where The River In My Heart Meets With The Sea 22

DIVERSITY RACE AND CULTURE

Taino Man 27
Looking Into The Mirror 28
Fear of The Unknown. 29
Hatred Seasons Hatred 30
Third World Parenting 31
Vanishing Small Towns 32
The Legacy Of A Brown-nosser 34
Welcome Home Stranger 35
He's Not A Home-Boy He Wasn't Born In My Hood 37
Celebration of Diversity (Just Let Them Play) 38
Freedom 40
Copan (A Mayan Resting Place) 41
Life's An Art. 42
Tribute to A Role Model 44
Yes…There Is Love (May Peace Prevail) poem 1:2 46
2:2 47
Tribute To A Role Model 48
A Sailor At Twenty Five 50
Hurricane Babies 51

At The Crack Of Dawn 52
Cardinal (A Well Oiled Hinge) 54
My Revival 56

SINGING ALOUD TO MY CHILDREN

Thanks For His Grace I Give 59
Tribute To A Gifted Artist 60
Dreaming About My Father 61
No Need To Dissolve A Fetus 63
A Song To Nikky (my number one Student) 65
Talking About Ma Boy (My # 1 athlete) 67
Mango Fever 68
He's Talking About Me 69
   by Sabas Whittaker lll (my son) 69
A Man With A Dream 70
   (by Sabas Whittaker lll) 70
A Song To Little Yannie
   (my favorite artist actress and musician) 71

LOVE AND ROMANCE

Desolate and Quiet Beach (1) 75
Lover In The Dark Midnight Sun (1) 76
Maiden Voyage 78
Abstract ll 79
I've Made A Promise 80
Abstract lll 82
The Scent Of A Love Impossible To Reach 83
The Meaning of Love 84
High On Love 85
Prisoners For Life Prisoners Through Love 86
Till Death Us Do Part 87
Was It Destiny 88
Espiritu Angelical 90

Your World	92
Sensual Beauty	93
The Calm After The Storm	95
Upon My Quest To Find Love	96
My African Queen	97
Earthly Eudimonia of Love	98
From My Heart To Your Heart	99
I Found A New Love	101
Thanks For Your Love.	103
Rekindle Love	104
Come On In	105
Capture My Soul And Make It Yours	106
If I Didn't Live Right	107
Broken Promises	108
Spiritual Guidance	109
Unconditional Love	110
Malnourished Love	112
Nightmare On Love Street	113
Holding On	114
Impression's Of A Blind, Blind Date	115
'Twas All About You	117
Abstract	118
My Lovers Home	120
Taino Man	122
Looking Into The Mirror	123
Poor Communication	124
Why The Hate	125
In Search of (Breaking Away)	126
Riding The Waves	127
Uxor Perfidia	129
The Death And Resurrection Of A Self Esteem	130
I Never Knew How Much Love Hurt	132
Without A Warning	133
Thought It Was Love	134
Scent of A Lost Love	135

I Remember You. Do you Remember Me? 136
I Have Lost Your Love 138
Forbidden Love 139
Is It A Rebound? 140
Nightmare On Love Street 141

LYRICS

A Song TO A Single Woman. 145
A Song To A Single Woman. 146
Love Could Find Us. 148
Tribute To A Vietnam Vet. 149
 Tribute To A Role Model. 150
My Revival. 151
A Communication With Life 152
You Send Your Son To Set Us Free 154
Tribute To A Homeless Vietnam Vet. 155
ALONE 157
DON'T LOOK DOWN ON YOUR BROTHER 159
A Song To Our Creator 161

SPIRITUALS

Hypocrisy 165
How Great Thou Art 166
Knock, Knock Knocking On Heavens Door 167
Abstract 169
Awareness 171

COMPREHENSION AWARENESS MINDFULNESS

No Need To Dissolve A Fetus (If I Just Listen And Follow
    Their Advice) 175
Cardinal (A Well Oiled Hinge) 178

Seaside Vision 180
A Father's Dreams, Prayers and Wishes (Consolation) 181
A Little Prayer 182
Betraying A Child (Thanks for the lesson) 183
A Song For All To Hear 185
Cocktail Of Vices 186
Solitary Journey 187
My Grandma 189
Life's Still An Art. 191
May Peace Prevail On Earth (Song) 193
The Art Of Caring 195
Revolution For Thy People. Whom? 196
ALONE 198
DON'T LOOK DOWN ON YOUR BROTHER
   (Song) 200
A Song To Our Creator 202
My Rival 204
A Communication With Life 205
You Send Your Son To Set Us Free 207
Tribute To A Homeless Vietnam Vet. 208
 Looking Back As Life Goes On. 210
Why The Hate 211
To My Homeless Neighbor 212
Either You, Either Me (My Homeless Neighbor) 214
Different Faces Different Ways
   (My Homeless Neighbor #2) 216
ALONE 217
Tribute To A Role Model 219
   Harvest 221
The Legacy Of A Brown-nosser 222
Tribute To A Role Model 223
YES…THERE IS LOVE (MAY PEACE PREVAIL)
   POEM 225
TRIBUTE TO A ROLE MODEL 227
Nightmare On Love Street 229

A COLLECTION OF SHORT STORIES, STORY LINES AND SYNOPSIS OF SCREEN AND STAGE PLAYS

Different Faces Different Ways 233
Mental Craze, Or Vogue. 235
Scopy's Journey 237
While I Was Praising the Lord 238
Hurricane Babies (Short Story) 242
FOREIGN EXCHANGE 246
FOREIGN EXCHANGE II 248
Synopsis 248
A Family Reunion At The Rally 250
An International Controversy. 252
Modern Times 253
Mundo Maya 254
To Sabas 255
   (by S. A. Brookter) 255
Words of Encouragement from My Friends,
   My Fans and My Critics. 257

I first give thanks to God, Our Heavenly Father for his inspiration, strength, courage and spirit given throughout this journey. A special thanks goes out to my loving sister, Esmeralda Whittaker de Romero for her inspiration and contribution to this body of work and to my niece Dr. Jaquelyn Richardson. I give thanks to my loving mother Neva and my sister Luisa for their love and courage always believing in me. And to my grand mother Irene Solomon Whittaker, may she rest in peace among all other angels for giving me such deep spiritual upbringing. Moreover for instilling in me at an early age that moral ethics, the value of hard work and the knowledge that freedom of speech and freedom of action, is meaningless without the freedom of knowing that there is no freedom of thought without external doubt, and the freedom of pleasure to reexamine such. This book is dedicated to all the strong women in my family. Thanks for giving me the breath of life.

PREFACE

Sabas Whittaker, has been writing poetry with spiritual meaning for more than 20 years. He began writing while on board the cargo and tanker ships as a young sailor on the high seas. He has now taken that passion for writing poems and incorporates it into his screen, stage plays and musicals. Inspiration taken with him from his extensive travels at sea and from the pain, and daily struggles he observed and experienced at firsthand by those who are daily stigmatized and ignored; while working in the mental health field and as volunteer with the various Anti Hunger and Anti Homeless Coalitions.

Mr. Whittaker, has also presented some of his work as a performing poet at the Warner Theater to benefit a homeless FISH shelter in Torrington, CT. He has opened for the New Jersey Mass Choir to benefit the Middlesex Aids Buddy Network, Middletown, CT and has performed at the Unitarian Fellowship to benefit The Hartford Ocotal Sister City Project's annual fund raiser, and has performed at Border's Book and Music to benefit GUIKIA, a bilingual performing art school in the city of Hartford CT. Sabas, has also performed his work in Washington D.C. At the International Poet's Society's, annual poetry award ceremony. Sabas Whittaker, is a member of the American Society of Composers Authors and Publishers ASCAP, since 1991.

ACKNOWLEDGMENTS

Therefore, great acknowledgment is given to all of those who have attempted to trample upon my dreams. I gave thanks to you for making me work a little harder and for contributing with such an extensive collection of real life anecdotes. Much respect and gratitude is given to the few who believed in me and encouraged me to carry on, and inspired me to write about what I've seen, what I've lived and what I've experienced. What was then negative, is now positive. It was all good, I have no regrets. A special thanks goes out to my coworkers for supporting, believing and cheering me on; specially to Michele Daniels, who basically read every page I placed in front of her and asked her to read, while requesting her opinion. A big thanks goes out also to Mr. Tony Yuskis for his words of encouragement and for sharing his writings, some of which inspired me to change my style of writing. Thanks guys, thanks for your faith, your prayers and your courage given. And to my good friend and buddy, Mr. Michael Boutin for hanging in there with me throughout the good and bad times; "You are a good friend… you're alike the brother I've always dreamt of having. Thanks." I must give thanks to my three children for their contribution, inspiration and motivation geared towards the completion of my collection. Thanks, to all you're all architects on board this cosmic, spiritual ride.

> "An artist must elect to fight for freedom or slavery
> I made my choice, I had no alternative"
> Paul Robeson

AUTOBIOGRAPHY

Sabas Whittaker, uses his pen to find peace, harmony and spirituality within. As a former merchant marine and law enforcement officer, now a composer, artist, stage and screen playwright, lyricist and poet. Sabas is often using the craft of writing painting and music as a metaphor for the examined and unexamined life, and cultures, while venturing with wry wisdom into the slow dawning awareness of our evanescence.

Throughout this body of work, he invites us to reexamine gentle regrets for time spent dabbling into failed dreams, while he rightfully describes, celebrates and claims passion for the spiritual and meaningful moments lived.

Sabas's, new collection of poetry Vestiges of A Journey, is creatively spiked with facts and the reality of our day to day living. And overflowing with feelings of joy, peace, harmony, sadness and the laughter with which we cloak our endeavors via the consequence of ignorant choices made on the pathway to our journey.

Vestiges of A Journey, is a creative collection of poems carefully crafted.

Sabas Whittaker was born in Honduras and his roots stem from African, British, American and West Indian lineage. Sabas, has also worked in the mental health field for the past 17 years and is currently employed as a Case Manager for the Department of Mental Health and Addictions Services.

MY GRANDMA

She spoke with such eloquence.
Words uttered daily as if she lived during
The Elizabethan times.
Muttering and expressing differences
commands request and orders
aloud in Queen's English.

Her long and woolly silver hair
in a long braid she carried.
With her long and pointy nose
she smelled from afar when her grand children
were in trouble.

A golden-oak complexion proudly displayed
as a monument to the mixture of cultures
flowing through her veins.
Part Jewish, part East Indian, part Scottish and part Black.

Alike a rainbow she embraced equality embodied
Which was spelled out among us
the beauty and importance of being diverse.
Difference ought not to exist in a lighter or darker shade.
But in the morals that one propagates.

Oh grandma… how I long for thine hugs, kisses
and words. Oh the scowling words.

Woe be unto you.

Her favorite words uttered in that sharp Elizabethan thong.
Which made us feel as if she were a living and walking
Shakespearean drama Queen.

When she reprimanded us
I rather received her lashes than to hear her powerful voice.
That's how much I loved and respected my grandma.

Sabas Whittaker © 1998

HAPPY MOTHER'S DAY

As we uttered the word mother from within our breath
enclosed we could feel the highest expression of love
for there's none other than her on this earth
to possess a nearer image to that of God's.

As we restlessly opened our eyes
to the radiant splendor of life
a mother's smiles and tears of joy awaits us
She tenderly holds us next to her heart
Her love pours it emanates for her new born child.

Sharing her love
giving most of herself
throughout all of our lives

She at times lays empty
like a deflated bag
while we walked around high
and ignoring her kisses as she gave us advice
How soon have we forgotten who give us the breath of life.

Sabas Whittaker © 2000

WHERE THE RIVER IN MY HEART MEETS WITH THE SEA

As I head down to the ocean once again to the mouth of the river where two mystical bodies becomes but one lonely they'll no longer remain for the horizon has brought together the skies to the sea our rainbow guides the rain.

For my mast stands tall, my sail's now full of wind our ship's on course and set to follow the brightest star.
She rocks back and fort as if awaiting the highest and most demanding wake.
The helm's well polished, the wind whistles such long awaited song to hear, her white sail's shaking as if dancing to the melody while the ocean provides the rhythm she bares.
From the ocean's salty mist to the tranquil brown face of my river breaking to the high seas my tall ship has once again taken.

As I head down to the river once again for the yearning of the running tide
A yearn for spirituality deep within, the call is clear, the call is wild, yet not to be denied.

My course now set
Her anchor's now lifted, all that I ask for is a windy day where the white clouds ought to be flying my souls been gifted.
From afar the sun begins to shine behind the mountain side an

eagle stands guard on her tallest mast upon my vessel's deck sea-gulls no longer cry but rather serves as escorts beckoning my arrival into our nearest port of call

As I head down to the river once again to the vagrant beach bum life I so long ago had left behind. Memories of a waterfront, wasted youth and drunken lonely nights remembered. Now all I ask is a merry yarn from a wondering fellow-sailor, a quiet place to rest my head for a sweet dream until this here long ordeal is over.

Sabas Whittaker

DIVERSITY RACE AND CULTURE

TAINO MAN

Oh bold Taino soldier
the children called you Tamaka
Great Indian chief

Though they thought you were extinct
told you had vanished off the face of the earth
Your son a living proof of your existence
testament of your courage and strength

You've returned to learn their books
their customs technology literature
while dwelling in the inner city's concrete jungles
Their wish were for you to remain enslaved
so that they could once again pissed upon your grave

Oh great Taino Man
you've once taken the sacred loin cloth of your ancestors
used it to separate veins
injecting into them misery disgrace and pain
created by those who have once pissed upon your ancestors grave

Wisdom knowledge and understanding
has brought you back afloat
Taino-Man
Great man of the East
Tamaka
long live the Indian chief

Sabas Whittaker 2000

LOOKING INTO THE MIRROR

As I look in the mirror
I feel as guilty as the white-man
for the destruction of my native brother's way of life
and my conscience still remains restless while at night

Should I be proud of great, great grand father's medals
won in battles during the Indian wars
when he for a couple of pieces of silver
engaged in the decimation and bloodshed of my fellowman
I asked myself.

A buffalo soldier on Wounded Knee
I'm fighting the Indian and getting paid to fight
even got myself a blue suit
no shoes yet, but I ain't no fool
Am fighting for freedom

He a savage
Got myself three of them today
even got me an army leave day with pay
Have a drink of gin its on me
bought a bottle when I pawned the medal earned
for scalping an Indian youth yesterday.

Sabas 2000

FEAR OF THE UNKNOWN.

By respecting differences between my brothers
I've learned how such could enriched my daily life.

Open… appreciate, rejoice in such diversity.
A richness brought to your land
an abundance in cultures foreign to your eyes and ears
not so long ago.

Engage me in dialog I beg
look me in the eyes and get to know me…
I want to get to know you.

Lets set aside prejudices
listen deeply and represent in truth.

I want to get to know you
I know you want to get to know me,
for I look and sound different
Yet I'm not afraid to love you.
Love… respect, understanding.

Ancestral voices heard at sunset
kept on telling me
that they're here to remind us
we owe to each other that much.
A love, respect and understanding
Spiritual debt long overdue
we owed to ourselves the human race

Sabas © 1998

HATRED SEASONS HATRED

Injured bird that stands between a rifle and a pointed arrow
motionless awaits and wonders who will be the first to shoot.
A direct aim
Wings spread wide, who will be the first to pierce his heart.

Trapped butterfly your wings being pulled apart.
Selfish evil ones attempting to destroy his very soul
and a love rooted deep within.

A belief on a truth that in the end will prevail
The love for thy children must come first.
Awake and walk the long hard road
on which no one cares.
Bethink
There is no hitchhiking allowed on this journey

Remember
Unwritten spiritual awakening
enabled my effort to survive.
Faith, spirituality and religious convictions
waned never to give up.
But to carry on.

Sabas © 1998

THIRD WORLD PARENTING

Does the act of giving birth earns her the right to be called a
   mother
The abuse of a right which lead to enslavement, extortion and
   manipulation
Come over here and take your whooping quietly
Don't you answer me back boy
for I will knock your teeth down into your throat

Let me procreate if I chose
I'll have all of those children that are sent my way
After all the eldest must help to care and provide for the young
Do not answer back I said
I am your parent and for that you must show gratitude.

I have brought enough sons here onto this earth
to take care of my every wish and need
though I haven't provided them with an education.
Boy, you should see how hard I had it.

Why save for the future
when I'm entitled a portion of their salary
to that I've already placed my demand
my offspring is my retirement plan.

Sabas © 1998

VANISHING SMALL TOWNS

With the horse and buggy my ancestors disembarked
The railroad came and I followed its tracks
an evolution in which the automobile now rules.
But from the pit of the clipper ship
I painted the landscape in my mind.

Adorned throughout your glory days
as a pageant beauty all dressed up
with no place to go during Christmas
or agricultural fairs

Little settlement that first began on a hilltop
slowly in time your expansion stretched along the water's edge
Great grandpa a former slave at the mill

Plaids of clustered villages eclipse
the rise an fall of a commodity
clothes pin, shoes, rocking chairs and buggy whips

A hike in the woods
cellar holes of farms that long ago failed
stand as a testament from those who came before
Monument of misery... poor restless souls.

Celebration of individualism
now a starve to the commons
The love for our cars and fashion
has far surpassed concern for our mountains

parks, playgrounds, natural habitat and public places

I've read the grace in your guide books
I am touched by echoes
reaching out from your historic walls and pillars

Sabas © 1998

THE LEGACY OF A BROWN-NOSSER

To he who carelessly laughs
at his neighbors expense
Who never consider non other than himself
but always awaits for someone else to take the fall
meanwhile he reaps the benefits

Fruit of labor
Labor of love
Now run to the boss
you've work hard for many years
mastering the skills of deceit

Sabas © 1998

WELCOME HOME STRANGER

I reminisce at times about the life I left behind
Happy days Happy nights
a laughter that still echoes in dreams
Memories of the good'old days
bright color pictures in my mind.

Exulted bliss of a childhood innocence
hangs like a melody that's being played in the wind
A souvenir whimsical chime
musical notes reference to a melodious past
Remembrance

In light of better days I've journeyed
The odd the bizarre the peculiar encountered
anchored vessel on foreign soil
in search of new adventures

Wrenching deep within my entrails
bittersweet sorrows of past misfortunes
now left behind in the abyss

I've brought fort in my mind a hope
The search the illusion of a new life
as I await to fulfill the dreams
pending within my soul.

Many nights I've cried myself to sleep
vigilance watchful alert
all disadvantages put aside.

Sabas © 1998

HE'S NOT A HOME-BOY HE WASN'T BORN IN MY HOOD

Oh young black man
you're sweet and docile
meek humble and mild.
You're the one with the great big smile
with the big-ole heart.
But you do have an accent
Beware my son.

Glitter of gold.
sparkle of silver…
decorative outlandish champagne and wine glasses
Remember to read the label before the contents is poured
abundance of spirits tends to produce backlashes.

Mild gush of wind which blows in cotton fields
or a quaint suburban gentle breeze.
Beware my son.
If it blows strong enough it could uproot trees.

My Negro-boy
you might be sweet and docile meek and mild
with great big heart and a big-ole smile
But you're still an outsider
and your accent still remains from afar.

Sabas Whittaker © 2000

CELEBRATION OF DIVERSITY
(JUST LET THEM PLAY)

The fear of entwined cultures
have us all at bay.
Sit outside the playground
hear the laughter listen to the sounds.

Look through your window
let us all learn... come with me experience the joy
As the wind blows, as we watch the children play

Find yourselves a quiet place
out there somewhere.
Take yourselves back in time to the land of make believe
and make yourselves at home

Sprawl along no longer in wild
as you find meaning
in the innocent laughs and screams

Relax!
They're just having fun, or perhaps
expanding their horizon and dreaming
of becoming our tomorrow's leaders.

Maybe by screaming out in laughter
they're at an early age settling
differences among cultures and races

that will arise.
Listen to their screams and cries
As they strengthen them
Viva la diversidad!

Sabas Whittaker

FREEDOM

The eagle in the bright blue sky
fly as high as the clouds,
fragile as a butterfly
his nature is so proud.

I saw the river running by
as the rain fell to the ground,
the sunset of my life goes shy;
among the growing crowds.

While standing by the shore of life,
I asked the living God.
Can I oh Lord reach the sky
just like the big flying bird?

I dream with fantasies of freedom,
still quietly reaching out my hands
trying to touch the blossom
beneath the living sands.

The waves of ocean dance along
the prisoners tears in the shadow.
The scream of children as a song
for freedom strikes on and on
like an arrow.

Sabas Whittaker (ASCAP)
Music composed by Sabas Whittaker
Sabas Copyright 1991 7/12/93

COPAN
(A MAYAN RESTING PLACE)

Resting slowly in time
history thought us you were asleep
Forgotten centuries of victory
a Mayan stands alone.

The colossal Olmec head
adorns your resting place,
like a father standing guard
near his son's bed post.

Mother Aztec bears her attitude,
as if observing a long lost child in wonders.
Vigilant cultures awaken
to tell the truth about a remnant tale of greed.

Sabas Whittaker © 97

LIFE'S AN ART.

From the ghettos of Central America,
while still holding on to a Honduran garbage can.
The tender age was eleven,
the stride to Costa Rica,
the dreams to become a productive man.

Ventured into unknown and remote lands,
a journey would then began.
Meager in physical appearance,
pigment of a skin to which many failed to grant their trust.

Unparalleled strong will and dreams to fulfill a thirst, and soothe a hunger for freedom on a journey that was almost lost in a third world dust.

Left alone into vast ocean, a drift, Satan's at the helm. Angels to his rescue.

Where is that friend, extend a hand.
Sole purpose of a goal,
yearned altruistic belief.
Prayers powerfully flowing from a bed ridden mother's mouth to her boy, a cross distant oceans; encouraging as they reach.

Prayers that during long travels through foreign lands to a weary and high spirited soul, His gospel brought relief.

Thus destined to follow a dream,
goals, struggle, spiritual growth.
Many encountered, many believed;
some even offered a free meal.
Hence without the sweat of his brow,
why such sweet deal.

Miles away laid a sick mother, grave afflictions burdened senses,
withered I am no more.
Anent a procreator, sole emptiness.
Heart full of joy rest steadfast at peace.

Sabas H. Whittaker © 1991

TRIBUTE TO A ROLE MODEL

He watched the days go by
as slow as winter
his heart beat was as loud as thunder

Behind steel bars he prayed, he wondered,
about the equal rights and justice
of his people once yanked from yonder.

Yet to those attempting to trash his dreams,
his freedom and his soul,
he showed no danger.

Dreams washed away,
like the sea washes the shore.
Freedom blown away,
like leaves during the fall season
after transposing into beautiful colors.
Yet even the bitter winter cold, still
failed to freeze his soul

Although many attempts
to tear him apart, with gospel and truth
he won their hearts.

A proper rout of life he helped us chart
and those born during a morality vacation,
he give his heart.

Like a shepherd he led his flock
toward the realization of un-accomplished dreams.
Freedom, equal rights and justice,
he was a native drive.

A father, a husband and a son at heart,
leaving behind such instruments of inspirations for peace.
This cruel world he then departs.

Sabas H. Whittaker (C 1991)

YES...THERE IS LOVE
(MAY PEACE PREVAIL)
POEM 1:2

To the soldier who strongly grasp his weapon
to fight in foreign land.
To the friend who uses cruel words
to doom his fellow man,
and to the son who still rebels in anger
and against his parents' love stands.

Please let me tell you
war is not the solution for peace...
mankind skirmish for self fulfillment and graft
only to end up with travails and grief.

Just shift your heart to a search.
Look around and ask yourselves?

 Why do the flowers in the gardens still grow in such lucid colors?
Why does the rain still fall and the sun continuously shines, despite
    of the abuse imposed upon our planet?
Why do trees still bear edible fruits
and oceans recover to
share their harvest, after they've been smeared with foreign refuse?
If there was no love.

The children implored
you restrain your selfishness

that you divert your sadness into laughter.
Shift your frown into a smile and let them know that there is love.

As world leaders to pause and foresee all of this great love.
Then please voice your story, because there is love.

So tear down the gates.
Remove the walls.
Dissolve the laws that chain us all
and let mankind for once stand tall.

Hence as foreigners to each other we stand.
Be vocal, ask your brothers, your neighbors, your sisters.
Yellow, brown, black, and white
to step forth and hold your hand.

2:2

And with one voice, one love, one harmony we'll shout, we'll sing.
Thank God almighty for giving us his love
May peace prevail
May peace prevail
 May peace prevail on Earth

Again we sing
Tear down the gates
Remove the walls.
Dissolve the laws that chain us all
and let mankind for once stand tall.

May peace prevail, may peace prevail,
May peace prevail on earth.

Sabas Whittaker © 1991

TRIBUTE TO A ROLE MODEL

He watched the days go by
as slow as winter
his heart beat was as loud as thunder

Behind steel bars he prayed, he wondered,
about the equal rights and justice
of his people once yanked from yonder.

Yet to those attempting to trash his dreams,
his freedom and his soul,
he showed no danger.

Dreams washed away,
like the sea washes the shore.
Freedom blown away,
like leaves during the fall season
after transposing into beautiful colors.
Yet even the bitter winter cold, still
failed to freeze his soul

Although many attempts
to tear him apart, with gospel and truth
he won their hearts.

A proper rout of life he helped us chart
and those born during a morality vacation,
he give his heart.

Like a shepherd he led his flock
toward the realization of un-accomplished dreams.
Freedom, equal rights and justice,
he was a native drive.

A father, a husband and a son at heart,
leaving behind such instruments of inspirations for peace.
This cruel world he then departs.

Sabas H. Whittaker © 1991

A SAILOR AT TWENTY FIVE

Alike his namesake in the old testament
forced to set a sail upon the turbulent waters
and save his life in the mid's of a tempest.

His mother and father, the quick thinking young couple
who swiftly placed their young son in a kitchen basin
and floated him down the river.
He was twenty five days old.

I tried to improvise with this makeshift vessel
Its made of Styrofoam, rubber and rope
my children will see tomorrow's sun rise.

A long lasting odyssey in the peaceful lake
where children's once played
now they die by its turbulent waters

Hear the screams, what a horrible dream
echoes which we rather soon forget
as we soon to return to smiles
He became the first modern sailor
at twenty five.

Sabas Whittaker © 1999

HURRICANE BABIES

Unfamiliar to the grasp of such tragedy
alike the rest of children throughout the world they play
Seminude they ran.
Diverting themselves in the stilled waters
Their laughter is heard in the rain.

Playful children throughout the day
whom at nightfall surrenders to exhaustion
Cold and still cleaving to the same wet clothing
carried on their backs for the past four days.

As in a form of protest
From their lips these words are uttered
(Food, Mama. Am hungry, mama)

Food, what food?
When we abandoned our home in search of a safe place
we left everything behind and underwater
We have not food, nor clothes
Everything was lost

But I still have my spirit
Thank God I still have my soul
I give thanks for sparing my little brother we can still play
we could still sing together now we could romp and roll.

Sabas © 1999

AT THE CRACK OF DAWN

At the crack of dawn
the sunlight spreads alike wildfire down the mountain
It illuminates as it shows my life now in disgrace.
Is it an apocalypse Perhaps
A prophecy a curse.

Home I had one yes
A once graceful expanse of red brick floors
adobe walls and endless gardens
now a cavity filled of barro

Vestiges of a daily life that rode the tide
of muddy waters down the mountain.

At the crack of dawn
the sunlight spreads alike wildfire down the mountain
Sadly a dream now lost.
My son now dreams of savoring a piece of tortillas
a bowl of rice, piece of chicharron, or a cup of beans.

At the crack of dawn
The sunlight spreads alike wildfire down the mountain
sadly the night has fallen and my son will again dream.

Though hungry
in his dreams he will again enjoy a plate of rice and beans, tortillas
and awakened in a struggle forcefully trying to retain the piece of
    chicharron between his little fingers.

At the crack of dawn
the sunlight spreads down the mountains alike wildfire
Perhaps illuminating our way into a new beginning.
At the crack of dawn.

Sabas Whittaker © 1999

CARDINAL
(A WELL OILED HINGE)

Alike the artist who seeks the beauty within his paintings
I tried to carve the wisdom in my pathway throughout life
living in a world where physical appearances are so valued
your inner spirit and your morals ignored.

1} Selfishness remains still our one main drive
Ti's a sole purpose in life to which we're tought
Selfishness remains still our one main drive
and to succeed at all cause we have learned.

2} Alike a Hitler's fallacy in his search for an Aryan race
we stand no better here today.
Why still remain slaves to the aesthetics
outer appearance and follow-fashion is your main.

3}Years of history has thought them nothing
nothing we've learned from our past
Years of history has thought us nothing
billions of bones lay forgotten in the dust.

Listen. Hear the sound of the gong
Follow carefully the sound of the bell
and observe where it leads your life.

Forget about who's eyes are bluer
who's boobs are bigger

who's hair is blondest, longest, thickest
Who has the highest Afro, the thinner, or thickest lips.
And who's skin is of a lighter or darker shade.
Listen, hear the madness!
And learn to discern the difference between vice and virtue.

MY REVIVAL

Amidst our harmony, exist a revival
so forceful, even storm failed to blow it away
Amidst our harmony, exist a revival
so forceful, even storm failed to blow it away

1}Lightening cannot, strike it down.
Strong winds cannot blow it away
Lightening cannot, strike it down.
Strong winds cannot blow it away

2}There's a deep settled peace within my soul
living where the healing water's flow
There's a deep settled peace within my soul
living where the healing water's flow

3}Hatred, grudge, nor anger can't stand in it's way
Peace, joy and happiness, that's my revival.
Fire won't consume, nor burned it away,
because its our revival.

Talked} There's a deep settled peace within my soul.
It's living where the healing water's flow.
There's a deep, deep settled peace within my soul
cascading where the healing water's flow.
Revive me, revive thy soul father
For I give thanks.

Sabas Whittaker © 1998 - 2000

SINGING ALOUD TO MY CHILDREN

THANKS FOR HIS GRACE I GIVE

God has gifted you with such special talent
that brings joy and smiles upon my face
The gift of art and wit
Communicate love and share his wonders literary vision
talented musical wisdom

Wouldn't it be wonderful to reach out and touch all those encountered
a simple greet in God's grace

To bring together artistic gifts we share
creating joy while delivering wow's ooh's and endless ahh's
as you send happiness their way

Not lets waste what God's has given
such special blessing shared in colors as you play
such beautiful melodious lyrics lift themselves of the page
before the instrument is sounded.

Uplifting stories that you tell
takes us back to days of child wonders and the land of make believe
A tear of joy is shed today I give thanks aloud in prayer
a stranger passed by the shop
he stop and bought my child's first painting

TRIBUTE TO A GIFTED ARTIST

(may you rest in peace, uncle Eddy)

Time of darkness fills the air around
when I think about his being gone
Though alone and with bare hands in such short time
you build so much.

How great you were plain and humble
so gifted warm and tender on sober days the art you shaped thought
    to create
When God's love danced within the joyfully glare of glittering
    eyes

You'd probably still teaching and painting
in heaven you must be
Though your memory in my work lives on

The thanks I give
for nothing built if not because of what he teach me

My heart still saddened may your spirit rest in peace
for alcohol and fast lane lifestyle
took you away from me when you were merely thirty three.

DREAMING ABOUT MY FATHER

Old -man sitting on a park bench
Sad eyes no smile
I paused and wondered while asking myself what did he do with his life
Did he ever thought about me about my life and if I either cried or smile
and was it hard to fulfill his selfish style.

Awfully sad to know he know lives in such a way
lonely and boring no friends to greet him no one talk with throughout the day
How lonely must he be
shades tree's bails of regrets now his only company

Though I can't help but smile with him
thus far he appears to be content
I'll pick him up and take him home give him warm meals
he could catch a nap and rest his tired bones watching tv in the lazy chair that's in my den. For at such age he's seen so much, his days now almost spent

Eyes opened sad twinkle no more glad
that lonely old man sad as he stands
each single day I'll take him home and feed him
he's no one other than my dad.

Hearty desires which in my mind and soul will linger on for ever spiritual journey that shaped and molded my manhood being into who I am today
To dream about what's not easily seeing
to give share provide yet not to await returns, nor give aid to regret for ten years ago my father really left for good and passed away around this date.

NO NEED TO DISSOLVE A FETUS

(If I Just Listen And Follow Their Advice)

Thirst for a child unquenched tortured and troubled couples paradise
Wait the stork do delivers newer baby's in your world, but wait for your time
Desire closed and surrender day to night rejoice to inner light thy strength

Wants fulfilled my vessel prepared still I thirst for the river not dried
Love of an innocence slowly to arrive thus fast passed by
Child born to a life on a long bent curve and winding roads trapped in a bubble for ever immune to a place in time which bast in ambivalent mood thus cry

Life proven false essence of fragrant love ignited by teenage passion and twisted hormonal flames yet luminous and thus mistaken for self esteem hence drawn on rapturous self claim.
From the deep perpetual wells so long a go dried yet occasionally filled during precise summer storms as incessant burst glow his whistling beacons her
to believe she's wrapped in the tender warmth of night, As she climbs through the window in disguise.
Rinsed through cleansing river of dreams a parent worst nightmare

by which she caries her failed inductment gain into the life long hall of fame
Between dreams caught among turbulent waves imprisoning heated gossip and lazy whispers of rundown neighborhoods in which she dwells. The grand marshal of his self proclaimed parade she will and still remains.

Reduced to the nothingness abound aberrant life now linked by the arms
of an over weight pushing fat harboring though still a teenager himself
Her lover and their four malnourished growing fast in mind and street wise wondering why where they were ever brought here.
Balls of funk driving through fuzzy circles and marching casual parades
Climbing unknown paths fulfilling with laughter the ego's of his homeboys wearing shorts bellow their ankles and untied tennis shoes. No belts just trying showoff their undies inch by inch sarcastically displaying favorite designer brand label. As they copy styles of convicts who's lives they've grown to envy

To the daughter who quit school and now stands in line awaiting a monthly ration of gobament cheese a wic voucher and food stamps. Her burden twice heavier moist air no longer dry to breath the consistent and carved ordained bickering she'd left behind on deaf ears everlastingly inundated in lost childhood tears
T'was her mom and dad who failed to give the good-old fashion advice now etched in a moment long after the fire the piece of pie carved for herself still lingers on as it slowly burns reminders in sadly regretful daily hints.
Painfully hidden behind colors to commit crimes upon the weak yet willing to disguise their assault under the banner and sanctity of culture
My sweet child if I fall in battle please don't just quit to chase the dream
Raise that flag and lead our courageous troop.

A SONG TO NIKKY
(MY NUMBER ONE STUDENT)

I found myself on a somewhat of an unfamiliar upward course
A beautiful child had just arrived your life now charted in the scope of my will The date her birth given was the thirteenth of April

Alike a beautiful rose you bloomed
Streaking alike such speed of light through my skies
and embracing each vain which flows blood to my heart with love and courage, you were born my brightest little star

Your love creating an escape from all which at the time were gloomy and doom. Your courage smiles and wit illuminated alike candles a dark room
Soothing my worldly traveled soul and filling my sphere with life's music
Your first cry a sweet little melody such beautiful and tender tune

Your angelical smile and spiritual growth then given harmonious tiny voice that beacons me in the right path to follow.
Each day I gave thanks for my new found everlasting love without such I'd been made weak irresponsible and shallow

Running away from the vessels and sea-weary family a pain such hard to bare Though running to you was the truth my life's first love true given
Watching you grow take your first steps said your first words little

angel from the heavens in prayer
Such meant more to me than any vessel upon a transatlantic voyage to which accustom I'd became so dare.

Though at times life had thrown such curbs. My beautiful little angel will continue to fly high to soar throughout the sky alike the singing birds.
First daughter of my heart first child first growing pain, you're in my blood which flows through my veins you are a part of me we'll hold each other's hand throughout the sun and rain.

TALKING ABOUT MA BOY (MY # 1 ATHLETE)

Once in a lifetime a man could truly consider himself fortunate
Twice if its a joyous arrival that touches his heart t'was the birth of my little boy now a compelling struggling energy consuming growing pain
But full of emotions and love

His interest is eating movies laughter and sports into the air he floats
Sailing away alike an eagle my boy though a 228 pound young man
Full of laughter and jokes to those encountered he is a supreme human being
Soft warm and nurturing he is a little teddy bear

Soothing well dressed and cool vibrating inner soul for which each day I'm proud and he's reminded of such turned out deep inspiration
To his little sister he now sings the lullaby's

Sketched deep in their stereo types I stepped into his life
Placing him on the rim of the fountain of life
Toasting and cheering on his touchdowns
As I remind him of the cold wall prison cells pathway to education and bad company which could easily turn his dreams to a frown

MANGO FEVER

I sat under the tree to await the fallen fruit as the wind blows
Reddish yellowish and green your colors are alike hanging rainbows
I give a gentle squeeze test and admire the heart like shape
and reminisce about a sweet child hood foot steps left behind in time
climbing neighbor hood trees to consume your delicious nectar

Taking a bite in my mouth and savoring the flavor of such tropical fruit
Delicious sweet delight juicy nut of my childhood paradise

By savoring and chewing slowly your wondrous pulp
I give thanks to natures gifts
The sun who's colors you so proudly display on your covers
The rain that irrigates the roots by which you bare
The fertile soil that feeds its nutrients you shared palatable delight
and to the wind which blows your leaves and brought you down to me
Take a bite is it ripe.

Taking a bite into my mouth and savoring the flavor of such tropical fruit
Delicious sweet delight juicy nut of my childhood paradise

HE'S TALKING ABOUT ME

by Sabas Whittaker lll (my son)

My dad is the one in room who talks a lot of junk
But he's no dummy he knows the funk
He's the man everyone loves to dump and trash upon
and the same old black nigga they all depend on

By many folks he was used and abused as a little boy
while taunting and dogging him alike an old used toy
My dad grew up with lots of hurt and pain
t'was then that he realized he needed something in his brain

Having a big house is nothing but taking care of your kids thus
assuring they'll grew up and on to something
So far its the best damn good coaching my dad can do
I'm fortunate and blessed to have a father like you

A MAN WITH A DREAM

(by Sabas Whittaker lll)

My dad grew up in a tenement yard poor ghetto an underprivileged child
In rat infested but morally upright dreaming of progress neighborhoods
That's why he made us kids a promise and told them not to worry he'll provide that to college they would

He told me you can make it without a wife
Now look at the old-man he appears to be set for life

With a boat a home lots of treaded brand name designs and a year model car; my oldie seemed to be living the life of a movie star
Surrounded by some of the bests of friends in the world who'd never need to asked him for a nickel a quarter nor a dime.

Most of my friends do not even have a wonderful dad like mine
They're almost all of either in hell or doing time.

In reality I didn't comprehend my dad did so much for me though now I see
I give my thanks for sharing his life and being a friend a coach and not just a dad by name
So when I grew I intent to make him proud and happy rather than sad
and bring him shame.

A SONG TO LITTLE YANNIE (MY FAVORITE ARTIST ACTRESS AND MUSICIAN)

Sweet butterfly that has appeared among my flower garden already in bloom
First discovered fighting through the small opening of a tiny cocoon
I sat and watched you grow as if forcing your body through an imaginary hole
yet without a struggle you rapidly appear bringing with you the keys to my soul.

I sat and listen I felt my heart skipping
The smoothness of your long fingers sliding across old piano keys in harmony
Sweet melody to create joy in your parents and siblings hearts
Through your tenderness my dreams pursued almost fulfilled
Beautiful child unknowingly our January new years gift

I find myself looking at her wondering and asking
Does she realize what talents lay inside dormant and barely awakened yet
I give a smile and share a hug with my tender little child
While I remind her of all the beauty she posses within
Not knowing what she's thinking but hangs her head in shy

I have faith in her fantastic gifts she'd given to share with all

thus my fear remains not far
for the simplicity within the beauty of her reality could make someone easily break her heart

Easily you then emerged to the open world though without a swollen head but wings to fly and attain your goals your limit the wide blue sky
Sweet butterfly at any moment your wings could become enlarge thus expanding to support your body in flight to remain free and follow the light
But when you land try landing within the lighted path on the runway.

LOVE AND ROMANCE

DESOLATE AND QUIET BEACH (1)

I love the bright sun and gentle breeze a Sunday afternoon ride
Warm and smooth sand a walk on a quiet beach holding hands
against my heart I placed mine onto your bosom
clean foams wash our footprints but leave the initialed hearts we've drawn in the sand
The rocks upon the shore stands awaiting the gentle waves for a shine
So that I can see the reflection in the moonlight of your smile

I feel your breathing alike a stream down my soul
Your sweet aroma the taste of your hot kisses alive remain in my mouth
While the sweat trickles down my spine and tickles my back
Your melting alike cream melts as my fingers search your gentle warmth in touch I search for the smooth silky garment
but found delicate wings of a butterfly Its oh so natural

Come angelical being, arrive with me.
Lets reach amount and aggregate our passion in ecstasy
Give me loving on this fiery afternoon
Sweet silk slipping entered in an up and down motion
Igniting your insides with passion and soothing our souls in amorous pleasures till I again await to satisfy our inner most desires on a Sunday afternoon.

LOVER IN THE DARK MIDNIGHT SUN (1)

I long for the day I'd lay and watch you sleep.
Echoes resounding in my mind about all the things I want to say
I wanted to shout aloud to the four points and tell the world
I'd fallen for someone I've yet to meet

Miles apart each night I await your call
I yearn to read your messages
such arrive alike stitches of golden silver thread to mend my heart
enclosing the joy within my soul
Its very sweet and yet so strange vogue and empty souls will find it
hard to understand and to believe

When I awake each morning I give thanks for those beautiful words
shared the night before and pray that we've not just uttered empty
words
solely to hear ourselves speak. Exchange thoughts tales and laughter
walking the path way in each of our lives

Since we've met through poetry
poetic lyrics written songs awaiting a jazz band composer to complete
the melody by which we'll soon dance
time and time I've given thanks for the literary gift and wisdom e
share, aid by which my loneliness is now long gone.
Missing you intensely at times yes though you're one click away

electro messages we've learned to hear our laughter and feel our smiles
modern tech to which am grateful happy moments shared in our lives

MAIDEN VOYAGE

Faintly I heard her calling alike an echo in the wind
I did not know her
Had never met her yet still I felt her love
Had never touched her nor have I heard her voice yet I detected her breathing
On each page and each line of each of her poems she beckoned my arrival into port

I drew a picture in my mind of what she could become in my heart
not a craving rather a longing for
Alike a blind sailor I pointed my vessel into uncharted waters
Without a red right returning buoy I embarked into an adventure

She'd always been there awaiting I then realized
disguised as a mother her beauty flourishing from within
her name adorning my vessel
her blissful gesture giving me the courage to carry on

The old piano keys are once again playing a melody
The flowers are once again blooming
The birds in the tree's are again singing
The ocean waves are dancing
The river looks alike a brand new old looking glass
All around appears as if being blessed with her song
I've been enabled again to yearn I'll carry on

ABSTRACT LL

Frustrated fractured and splintered broken heart
cracked like a shell in a million pieces and thrown on the floor
inclined to give it up and run her pain easily shown through her walk
As a friend I stepped on in to help her find her way perhaps not thinking

with provocation her hurt began to unbind
loosening its grip onto my reality awakened
to the feelings odd and strange she were then in my life
My hearty sad and simple way of living now quickly subject to change

beating with joy pulsating with love so long ago foreign
kissed minted imagination from vivid pictures of dreams
prayers to silently course to fears never to hold
streams of tears flowing East in search for the rising sun
shimmering in the glittering light of thawed out emotions
new dreams then easily became

I'VE MADE A PROMISE

Kiss me hard for we're about to embark on a start
romance that'll lead so deep
Awake me from such long nightmare and rest my heart asleep

Lay next to me and hold thy heart carefully for which its fragile
elevate me to an ecstasy that soothes, desires yet so magic
Let your love overflow within for I am blind though burlier in
appearance
Warm thou winters with soothing touch of burning fire
surrendered heat in passions of desire

Rest upon my chest and hear my heavy breathing
Each basely breath appear
alike a dancing instrument whispering in the wind and professing
my love alike a blossoming garden trying to touch the sun
Hence such difference this time around simple even smooth and
steady
Not too fast I have no haste I'll await until you're ready

I watched her stand and saw her smile
Softly reaching and looking up at the stars
as if searching for assurance in what we now share
alike a flower blossom reaching for the sun during spring

Sing sweet melody to my window my little bird for it's only rain storms which follow us around and sometimes comes with pain I'll kiss your tears and wipe your eyes weep no longer in vain For its your song that naturally plays rejoice in choir of angels bring fort fruits of love and joy awake us from such long nightmare to rest we've placed our sorrows.

ABSTRACT LLL

Walk with me and hold my hand as if we were the only souls ones on this great land
Lay next to me and tell me your inner most secrets talk to me reveal your dreams rid yourself of all burdens carried within just for a moment be free

Look at me unafraid, who not I.
allow yourself to set free
Unleash society given chains to your birthright
Let love out for all to hear loud shouts

Not thou run in shame no longer lead whom to be your judge
a lie discussed with such disgust as if you've entered judgment day
lived thy life thus end the game simply because

THE SCENT OF A LOVE IMPOSSIBLE TO REACH

Candid flowers exotic gardens
harmonious morning, sweet smell of spring
Oh eternal love immortally yours
surrendered I am at your feet.

Heart, spirit and soul
an open book for all to read.
Just another chapter
Perhaps now just yesterday's news.

Butterfly in the field
rhythm of radiant sunshine
that beams your every move
Fly...
I will follow you in my dreams

Embellished enchanted beauty.
Your wings...
Their colors an inspiration of love
Nautical waves on which
my silent love remains adrift.

Sabas Whittaker © 1998

THE MEANING OF LOVE

'Twas in search for the meaning of love when I realized that
Mindfulness, altruism and the holly spirit were all agents of healing.

That when you have altruism in your heart you have understanding
When you have understanding you have a covenant an agreement to agree.
Surrender

Sound at heart, spiritually grounded.
Mindfulness was the key to love, love was the way,
The way to the holy spirit, the way to understanding
that we can heal the wounds in our minds, soul, heart and spirit

I've found the meaning of true love.
But the search for peace remains alive and well.

Sabas © 1998

HIGH ON LOVE

Alike the male humming bird I will swoop in figure eight
until an impressed female joins my flight
Together we'll soar to a hundred feet in the skies.

Dream on
for I cannot reach such heights in flight
for I will forever carry you deep within in my heart
Eternally

Inspired by courtship dances
a face which perfectly matched my love map
body language appeasing to my soul mate
Romantic partner

A kiss The meaning of two people so close
one cannot see nor find anything wrong with the other
Love

An addiction a high an early infatuation
a chemical release that allows us to go for long periods
without the need for food nor sleep

Together we soar
as we try to accomplish our dreams
A ride to infinity.

Sabas Whittaker © 1998

PRISONERS FOR LIFE
PRISONERS THROUGH LOVE

She stands affront a large steel gate
ramshackle burdened down in life
The weight of sorrows now a pain which cuts her breathing
A loneliness she still not dare to admit
in spite

Wondering eyes focused on the outer sphere
as if searching through infinity for a failed dream.
Lost deep in thought
Anchored vision on the memory of an infallible love
Affection gone sadly and tragically in disharmony
She has no remedy he remains behind bars.

Freedom... justice, equality
How much longer must you come to visit
What must she do to reinvent the form
in which to gather the necessary money
to finally get her lover out of prison.

In her mind he remains innocent
still claiming it was in self defense.

Sabas Whittaker © 1998

TILL DEATH US DO PART

Throughout the years they walked in a daze
without holding each others hands
two souls lost deep in their own thoughts.

But still tried to look into each others hearts
And found two set of eyes lost into the deep blue yonder
as if in search for the promise of something better

The share of a sentiment
measured details captured into their minds
Comparison of cultural values
tenderness drained by social demands

Across the years they walk
never to hold each others hands
Lost in thought daze mystification
perhaps too busy fighting their own demons
Once in the heavens will you walk with him
will you hold his hand.

                              Sabas Whittaker © 1998

WAS IT DESTINY

I saw her for the first time in he mall
our eyes made contact, we shook hands
we were introduced. She wore a yellow top
faded blue jeans and white leather sneakers

I watched her smooth lips as they moved
during conversation
My first thought
God she must be a great kisser!

A radiant smile we shared
as if she read my mind I was shy and I blush
I was in the company of my adulterous wife.

On our second encounter
a crowded super market parking lot
I smiled, she winked.
Casual greeting we each headed our way
I still remember what she wore
I don't even have to think.

Months later we worked the same shift
eight long hours might I add
I was asked to work a double
she then worked her regular third shift
Usually a long day, but she was there
It seemed too short of a time
Where have all the hours gone.

We talk, we smiled nothing deep, nothing serious
All superficial stuff
Yet almost five years later
I still remember every word, her radiant splendid smile
She asked about me later
I was still married with a wife who was seeking counseling at the
    time

Casual encounter in a crowded place
A hug which came from the heart
She wore a red woolen sweater, tight fitted jeans
and a fragrance which still penetrates
The thought alone is soothing
'twas almost eight years ago

Now divorced a clamor from my heart
to seek her out burns within my deepest.
The desire still strongly awake in my heart
Is it an intuition, unsuspicious loved encountered.
Perhaps a mere fantasy

Sabas Whittaker © 1998

ESPIRITU ANGELICAL

I thank the almighty for the inspiration given
Ability to love and create love
Wisdom of a judgment
a melody in song that soothes our soul

When down you came around
picture perfect spirit of an angel
from afar keeps a watchful eye
While am awake at day or as I sleep at night

Though we have yet to meet in the flesh
pathway of two lives linked via our letters,
photographs and thoughts
Blessed be thy shared admiration
Essence of souls connected in harmony.

For the breath of life each day I give thanks
Each day I pray our dance will come to fruition
a ceremony in which we hold hands a walk a talk
As our eyes though closed gaze deep into our inner-self
to find meaning in our existence.

I whispered in the wind my sweet
angel's name.
Echo that still resounds in my heart
you are the one, you are not the many.
My angel… my sweet and beautiful friend.

A shared love carried throughout our journey
profound harmony sentimental reasoning to our souls
by which in joy I give thanks to God's genius inspiration
A technology by which we've met.
May He bless and guide you
May He bless our souls, journeying throughout
this vast Internet

Sabas ©

YOUR WORLD

I want to be your dream
your wish and your fantasy
I want to climb high and ride the highest mountain
I want to touch, I want to reach, I want to grab
I want to give if I could, I want to give my lover the skies.

I scream and yelled… I called your name out loud
into the wide blue yonder
while I tried to reach and grab, reach and grab
for the brightest star.

But as for now all I could give is my heart
All that I could spare is my soul, my spirit, my being
And my everything replenished with love.

Star gasser, star gasser
would you help me reach the skies
Would you help me find the biggest and brightest star
I want to wrapped it and placed it near my lovers heart

I want to be your dream
your wish, your fantasy
I want to climb high and ride the highest mountain
I want to touch, I want to reach, I want to float among the clouds.
I want to give my lover the sky, the moon, the sun.
I want to be her world for she's already mine.

Sabas Whittaker ©

SENSUAL BEAUTY

A morning smile awakened
Fresh taste in thine mouth
Amorous kiss received.

I lay in bed eyes closed
to visualize your smiling face.

Your spirit. A work of art
One by which tribesmen throughout the world
partake in shaping image

Your body
Sculpted by ancestral kings and gods
Envisioned the golden chisel of Pharoah as he carefully
chipped away each contour in shape
The carving knife in Noktezuma skillful hands
defines your radiance still ignored.

In your eyes you carry the sensual beauty of Cleopatra's erotic
    conquest
and the delicate touch of Nephertiti our mother queen
A spirit as strong in speech to silence the Greek gods in pause
Your poetry, philosophy and wit
A knowledge of life.
Wisdom to love you've thought
and is so well received.

On a cold January evening I first heard your name
'twas then my heart suddenly alive became
On that rainy night in June we met
as if such were sent from the heavens
to wash away our torrid past
and pave with harmony, joy and splendor
the pathway to a new beginning

A morning smile awaken
still savoring sweet taste of last night's kisses
the smell of fresh cut flowers
adorned with splendor.

Good morning sunshine good morning love
song bird of grace that to my window
 brought a melody of peace for two.

Sabas Whittaker © 98

THE CALM AFTER THE STORM

Good morning songbird
Awakened early once again
to sing the songs of a new beginning.

Silenced in time by vouchers
threatening your soul and spirit
they dreaded your peaceful song.
Be still and sing.
Remain ahead of the game.

Good morning songbird
let us welcome this new day.

They may even reposes material things
but fall short to capture your soul and spirit
as they fail to destroy your hopes, your dreams.

Your spirit will emerge stronger
triumphantly you stand
As the spirit of Solomon protects you from the rain.

Good morning songbird
awake and sing…
Though its winter
your anointed soul will make believe its spring.

Sabas Whittaker © 98

UPON MY QUEST TO FIND LOVE

Befall in the season on a day
In Southern ways on a taboo do they lay
Ready to wenden on my pilgrimage
Oh, Magistrate with full devout courage
night turned into hostility.
Onward move forward with full rise
we'll make our way there as devise.

Our two souls therefore which are one
though I must go endure not yet a breach
But an expansion to airy thinness beat.

If they be two, they are two so
as stiff twin compasses are two
Thy soul the fix foot makes no show to move
But doth remains in doubt if others do.

Sabas Whittaker © 98

MY AFRICAN QUEEN

Her skin is as dark as ebony
A smile as wide as the river Nile.
Nature's sweet cinnamon
beautiful African child.

A courage, strength and endurance
to outlast the pyramids.
Spiritual radiance brighter than any sunshine seen.
With her presence she'll light the darkest of rooms
and breathe life into the dullest of gatherings.

To be a direct descendant of Kunta Quinte
is her only claim.
Though the spirit of Shacka Zulu, Haile Selasy
Marcus Garvey, Harriet Tubman
Swahili and Mandingo blood alike rivers
flows through her veins

With her ivory smile she could initiate
an open dialog with creatures big and small in the wild.
Voicing out-most respect and concern for all living beings
My beautiful, my princess, my African Queen.

Sabas Whittaker © 98

EARTHLY EUDIMONIA OF LOVE

Your flourish comes from within
they may not know it
to selfish ones you never showed it.

Inner beauty which rest steadfast upon your heart,
the day we met I knew it from the start.
When we're together I'm alive
ardent love, splendid smile.
Oh strengthened drive.

Fretting nigh, thine superficial appearances
encountered.
Ignored peaceful harmony, joyful steps in your dance.
The tender look in your dark brown eyes
makes me feel like a little boy, who has stumbled
upon his favorite toy.

Communion which flows like crystal waters,
cascading freely upon our souls.
I've drunk from your well of love to intoxicate.

Oh togetherness and trust, let our love remain.
Spiritual, faith linked like a chain.

Sabas H. Whittaker © 1996

FROM MY HEART TO YOUR HEART

{Only My Heart Knows}

Only my heart knows
how much you mean to me.
I wonder if it shows
how hard I've tried
to proved my love

And each and every night
I go to sleep I dream of you
and oh how good it feels
to know it's you
who are in my dreams

From my heart to your heart
fill with such love we have no need.
From my heart to your heart
and all of this joy
we've ought to feel

I wonder if you felt
the way I did when we first kiss?
And I thank my lucky stars
to know that soon
you will be my wife

I have prayed for some one special
to give my love and share my dream
you are in my heart baby
you're in my heart
And that's a very good start

   Talked (rap style)
Only my heart knows,
how much you mean to me
and oh how great is my love for you.
Now on my knees I pray to God,
for better avenues
to prove and to show you;
in more than a thousand ways
how much I love you and how happy
I am at your side.

Because just with the thought
of having you on my mind, turns me on
and into the most fortunate men on Earth.
Now am just waiting for the moment,
just waiting for the day,
waiting for the right time;
when our hearts become
one rhythm of love.
then I'll loudly shout to the world
I love you

   Lyrics and music by Sabas H. Whittaker (ASCAP)
   Copyright 1991 from the album Solo Mi Corazon (Only My Heart Knows)

I FOUND A NEW LOVE

I found a friend, who'll care until the end
To her, I have nothing to prove, but love
all that she wanted from me, is to show that
I'll care that I'll show self respect.

Someone
whom I don't even have to impress
because her love, her soul and her spirit,
My sweet Lord, has already blessed

I found a friend, that said she cared.
and that by my right side,
she'll always be there.

I've asked my good Lord, is this a blessing?
You're both are single, I don't see the sin.
Dance, go right ahead and mingle.

Today I've entered into my father's presence,
I think he herd when I prayed, shout and sing.
I found a friend, who said she cared
and by my side swore to always be there.

This proves true love
and I know to love her.
I've proved to love
And I'll live to love her

We showed our love
Her soul as peaceful as that of a dove's
She filled my heart, with joy and glory
Listened closely to my songs.
While longwindedly I gladly repeated my story.

Sabas H. Whittaker ©

THANKS FOR YOUR LOVE.

I thank the almighty God,
for his genius inspiration.
A sheared love carried deep within my heart,
profound joy in my soul.

How could I, describe with words my feelings?
Its pure... oh, you can be sure!
So full of truth and so divine,
its like a new day sunshine.

A like the arrival of spring
upon still frozen lakes,
after a long cold winter.

I know its easy to say I love you,
but it's hard to love the way I love you,
since its so easy to say I love you,
why is it so hard for you to do?

With broken heart, I'll thank the almighty God
for his love buried deep within my soul.
Inspiration shared with you in my song,
harmony of angelical melody delivered in motion.

Sabas Whittaker © 1991

REKINDLE LOVE

Someone dear to his heart walked away
His soul-mate drifted off today
And it tore him apart.

I laid in bed enjoying her sunrise
as she enjoyed mine.
As if to tarnish our bright sky
a phone-call came in.

Darkened clouds rolled across
And our rainbow disappear.

Key in ignition
Tires burning
she speeded down the old driveway
Sat by the phone awaiting a call that were not to come

Attempted to call, got answering machine
fourteen messages still remain
heart which cries out her lost just the same

Lets just all commiserate
and bury for once that sadness
Have a spirit, enjoy... lets celebrate.

Sabas Whittaker © 98

COME ON IN

You stepped into my life
like water flowing down endless streams.
Showered me with indulgence, love, joy,
happiness.
As if experiencing a dream
from which I was afraid to awaken

High pitch singing of birds
Rustling of trees in the wind
Gallivanting of forest duelers in pairs
All served as a reminder that you were here
that it wasn't just a dream
that you do exist.

Because your love is all around
Alike raindrops pouring into a crystal bowl
your love cascaded all down my soul

I now rejoice and celebrate
if its all a dream in which am deeply immersed
No. I really don't want to ever awake.

Though eyes closed my heart tells me its real
My senses detect, they feel.
Oh, yeah!
It is real
In love I do believe.

Sabas Whittaker © 1998

CAPTURE MY SOUL
AND MAKE IT YOURS

Seize my soul and indulge
why don't you.
Drunken my spirit to intoxicate
then love me until craze.

Awaken my dreams with your presence
Startle my fears with your light
something about you makes it feel just right.

Capture my soul why don't you
Elevate and keep me my spirit high
For I've drank from your soul from your fountain
intoxicated with love I followed your light.

You've captured my soul in a harvest
Now plant it somewhere near your heart
and let your spirit irrigate it with gathered clouds of passion.

Undress my soul why don't you
let us indulge in one another to intoxicate
as we make love to each other until craze.

Sabas Whittaker © 1998

IF I DIDN'T LIVE RIGHT

I'd be nailed to a bar stool
confiding all of my mishap and my deepest to unknown faces
while I toast my failed journeys with strangers.
My bartender pretends to listen as he pours my drink.

The going rate for my psychiatrist
A dollar fifty plus the tip
Abandonment of oneself
sucking down Wild Turkey whisky and gin to help discount my
    pass
forget her face and shake off my pain and sorrow.
I've tried to drown but they could both swim.

Where are you now blessed soul
Where are you hidden
Open up your heart just a little and let me in
Open up your soul and understand.

Rescue me from this ocean
for I am wounded and drowning in desperation
An inebriated crying rage on a barstool
the bar tender knows my story by heart
as I toast my misfortunes with unknown faces
Thank God another night has drifted by.

Sabas Whittaker © 1998

BROKEN PROMISES

As we remember the first lines of that sweet old song, Members Only Tonight, Don't Need No Money To Qualify, all you must bring to the party with you is your broken heart. In this segment, we celebrate broken promises. And dedicated it to all who's heart has broken and cheated on at some point in their lives.

Do not ever make yourself bitter, because those who have created your pain want you to become angry, bitter, hurtful and mean. It is what gives them the satisfaction and its also indication that they have won and all at your expense. Do not hate them, but rather love them and smile when you see them, because God placed them in your way as a hurdle so that you can learn to jump over them and make it to the finish line of happiness and bring home the gold. Just go on bout your business and make yourself sweet for the other person who comes around in your life, and treat them twice as good as the one before. Move on, life is too short sweet and beautiful to remain stagnant, alike still waters settled into a puddle in some back alley; behind the old-speak easy. Lift your head off the bar and drop not another quarter into that old-jukebox I said!

Pick up the pieces!

SPIRITUAL GUIDANCE

Throughout life's journey wrong choices were made
Encountered souls of lesser care
So full of vengeance and crude hate

Was it God's choice perhaps
For I to stumble upon a few wrong ones
Before meeting Mrs. Wright
A grateful gesture wonderful gift received
the thanks for his blessings given each day.

For I stood outside the closed doors to happiness
too long awaited while ignoring
Others had been opened awaiting my presence

In grand pa's own words uttered
One never know what we really had
until its gone
While my inner spirit respond
One never know what has been missing
until it arrives

Be open to others
Give a chance a dance
Be ye not as the horse, or as the mule
Which have no understanding
And who's mouth must be held in
with a bit and bridle less they come near unto the

Sabas Whittaker © 2000

UNCONDITIONAL LOVE

Give your love
Don't await for assurance that they'll love you in return
Just sit and wait for it to grow in their hearts
And if it doesn't show content for has grown in yours

We betray one another
While ridding high on the aesthetic gleam
As we continue to ignore that in our quest for love
Looks can be deceiving
Wealth can be spent gambled away or faded
But the smile in the hearths of those
Considered to be not so handsome
Is of a lifetime inner spirit and strength

Bring forth your happiness
Enjoy your dance
Make yourself sweet it doesn't have to be romance

Vestiges left behind
As I followed in your pathway
relishing in happiness and joy
are those who have cried
those who have hurt
those who have searched
and those who have tried

For love begins with a smile
grows with a kiss
and ends with in hurtful bails pain and tears

We cannot place condition on love
Nor on those who love us
They're only trying to learn us
For yet we do not quite know ourselves
But expect to judge in full knowledge
Love ougth to shape us
into instruments of peace and fellowship
love ougth to help us
cease from anger and forsake wrath.
And to fret not thyself in any wise to do evil

Sabas Whittaker © 2000

MALNOURISHED LOVE

Outside the rain keeps falling
inside her heart still pounds
he walks away
On a train bound to nowhere he now rides

Nurture
A love that fell short to everlastingness and promises
Gardens where once amorous, ardent passions bloomed
withered fields now stand to erode
distanced and wide apart from each other.

Outside the rain still falls
she dreams on his return
Wide awake into the night a watchful eye she keeps.
Hear the weep of lamentation.
I heard her sob last night
She shows a strong Latino women charm
her spirit remains still high.

Outside the rain keeps falling
turbulence now rest steadfast
The train reaches the station
is it the end of the ride
Final destination

Right across the street stands the old train station
At her front door he disembarks

Sabas © 1998

NIGHTMARE ON LOVE STREET

Winds whistling through a window pane
inside a restless soul lays asleep.
Briskly awakened by the dreams of a lost heart
as if being pricked by a thorn broken
off of a dried rose stem.

Fidelity, cardinal devotion
linked to an aura now dimmed.
Ardor silenced quietly throughout the night.
Journey on sunsets now traded in.

Uncertainties
plunged thyself into a stormy life.
Be free to set a sail in pursuit of a long overdue
Happiness, joy and laughter
Like a scream echoing throughout the dark.
There is an end
I've seen the light of courage.
    I've broken away from the chains of pain
And now I move on

Goodbye selfishness, hello happiness
Now I walk on by bout my business
Big smile on my face

Sabas Whittaker © 2000

HOLDING ON

I hold on to the memory
As I walk around throughout the night
Of another love that came and disappear in a flash of light

What have they to say about you
what imperfections doesn't they like
Just another one who tried to change you
mold you drain and use you
for pure pleasure and delight

I hold on to the memory
as I ride through the pitch dark and desolate night
on a boulevard yet crowded and dazzling with thousands of lights
    wondering to myself
what dimmed bulb stands awaiting
for this fool to re-illuminate them
and let them once again stand bright

Sabas Whittaker 2000

IMPRESSION'S OF A BLIND, BLIND DATE

this was supposed to be harmonious I'd been told you were educated and somewhat civilized. Though I wasn't expecting to meet an angel
I gave you nothing but unconditional love, respect and praises
Introduced for the first time to a dignified upright way of living and self respect given.
Your head got swell exposing the warp side of uncovered layers as you fled.
Into the jesuit commune down the road I now seek refuge, perhaps hiding and still running from your twisted evil lies.

I didn't set search to find an enemy
we were supposed to meet just down the hall, have diner, share a drink, laughter perhaps a dance and a smile
The priest's at the alter dusting the cynicism from his chosen profession
To societies rules we must show credence marriage a final motivator which would've ended in disgrace.

i breathe now free and i no longer wonder
no, i do not wonder for i give thanks for simply being blessed with a proactive and creative mind to think
the air around here no longer speak squabble I give no apologies for being a modern man for within my new life all is cohesion welcome poetry the music that is word

No longer am I moved by sea changes nor manipulations from a beast
Rather my desires to float above all that stifles and remain a soul well grounded in spirituality as I travel in search for peace.

I first listened with closed eyes searching for the music in your word
needing a few swipes of cynicism before reality finally opened my mind
sacrificing several months and several dollars before putting you out of my heart and mind and forever out to sea.

'TWAS ALL ABOUT YOU

A pauper at your feet yes that I almost became
I could've been a larvae with a very low self-esteem
As a disgusting slime you saw me while you ignored and made mockery of my foreign origin
Turning your head away as I pleaded my case
Shouting aloud in an inner tenement ghetto fashion
I placed my pride aside and pleaded for your understanding and compassion
You could hear, but instead uttered words popping in thin air
Snapping your fingers bopping your head as if you were the original miss thang. I later came to realize that yes you were really miss something-else

Tied still at your ankles I tried to shake loose codependent and affixed
You Kept on moving dismissive head high
My sight was never worthy for your eyes
But rather to furnish your outlandish living style
moments spent together were wasted time to soothe your selfish crave

Pause your thoughts cease your hate Slow your mind and hear me
See though a male black foreigner am still a human being
my heart still listens and it does feel.

ABSTRACT

Were you chosen to dissect my life I asked
Interviews analysis and question about
common stories we all drag behind which ought to be told
Instead in silence wondered hold
As if to tell ourselves
We cannot change what's already unfold

We have no impact on what will be the outcome of facts already given
A reality that's based on perception and not truth, nor intuition
rather ill treated and maladapted mindset of advise taken from the selfish
Just because jealousy perhaps I wonder

As I stepped into the light 'twas the light of reason
Not that which makes us such an overnight success
I've stood in dress rehearsal for many of years
Bare feet empty stomach hopeless not a smile but tears and came face to face with fears to overcome battles lost
Thus the cost paid was high hence to succeed not just survive

Some people will ask why are you in such high position
Why not I then asked We've all been given the same opportunity some perhaps even more thus quantity isn't the main
To follow our dream and follow our purpose in life
Alike a salmon we're born to swim upstream
but life is difficult and realizing it difficult it'll remain
Though foolish empty and selfish souls will choose to live a lie and

eventually die in vain merely to feed an illusion and follow a crowd unable to show their gain

Will you now stand tall and proud will you follow your heart
Will you have the courage to answer His call
You can't find God in a bottle or battle your demons with your vice
He's going to find you if you live an upright you'd be led by the Spirit
Learn to focus the true meaning of your life
Healed from within and all doubt will disappear to a happy way of living you will no longer fear

Temptations always lurk in the shadows to challenge
Your faith to fight for what you believe when you're led by the spirit
You can't conceive conceding A battle already won
The Son of God the Holy Spirit mindfulness and altruism are to remain the chosen way of life

MY LOVERS HOME

(I Hang With Disrespect and Disregard)

Within my crave for the aesthetic gleam I've lost my wit
as I tapped on emotions dreams and empty promises of false adventures
Harboring layers of mundane and well spoken bleary dreams
drained souls and spiritually empty shells

One by one they came to the parties and banquets I could not afford
They ate and drank and often cleaned their plates while requesting for a take home. In such swift move grasping at your soul and spirit.
Never ceasing they kept on showing up in droves confounded friendship and kindness largely abused

I stood in the mirror and watched my life slipping by
Gossip music chatter, cannabis and alcohol wasn't my long awaited search for a piece of the pie
Dreams swiftly turning into unvirtuous nightmares
wild parties and her drunken stupor now a daily vice.
Closed places opened wounds yield now to bleeding hate
self love was the darkened bridge on which they'll all continue their travels

The breath of time wink my star to arrive
the sun led my shadow to awakened senses on time
I stood the challenge I survived your wrath oh selfish confidants

I've learned to know and love the real me
I had long ago been ready to know and meet the real you
Now in the sun I glow
no longer in need of such, but knowledge wit and enriched self esteem

TAINO MAN

Oh bold Taino soldier
the children called you Tamaka
Great Indian chief

Though they thought you were extinct
told you had vanished off the face of the earth
Your son a living proof of your existence
testament of your courage and strength

You've returned to learn their books
their customs technology literature
while dwelling in the inner city's concrete jungles
Their wish were for you to remain enslaved
so that they could once again pissed upon your grave

Oh great Taino Man
you've once taken the sacred the loin cloth of your ancestors
used it to separate veins
injecting into them misery disgrace and pain
created by those who have once pissed upon your ancestors grave

Wisdom knowledge and understanding
has brought you back afloat
Taino-Man
Great man of the East
Tamaka
long live the Indian chief

Sabas Whittaker 2000

LOOKING INTO THE MIRROR

As I look in the mirror
I feel as guilty as the white-man
for the destruction of my native brother's way of life
and my conscience still remains restless while at night

Should I be proud of great, great grand father's medals
won in battles during the Indian wars
when he for a couple of pieces of silver
engaged in the decimation and bloodshed of my fellowman
I asked myself.

A buffalo soldier on Wounded Knee
I'm fighting the Indian and getting paid to fight
even got myself a blue suit
no shoes yet, but I ain't no fool
Am fighting for freedom

He a savage
Got myself three of them today
even got me an army leave day with pay
Have a drink of gin its on me
bought a bottle when I pawned the medal earned
for scalping an Indian youth yesterday.

Sabas 2000

POOR COMMUNICATION

The light on my caller ID blinks no more
Your voice is no longer heard on my answering machine
Is it the end of our dream.
Perhaps the beginning and the end of a new journey

Playgrounds in which we once
Amorously giggle hold hands
ran and acted like children
now ghostly quiet they stand
The rusted chains abandoned only remains

The light on my caller ID
Blinks no more
Is it the end of the rain The storm
I guess I've gotten used
To no longer hearing your voice
On my answering machine

Am once again in control of my destiny
My plans my future and all dreams

Sabas Whittaker 2000

WHY THE HATE

When we hate
Hatred builds a wall around us
At first we learn to hate the enemy
Then we hate the neighbor
Then our friends
Then our children
Then our brother sister and parents
And when we have no one else to hate
We began to hate ourselves

My heart and soul remains free
Of hatred toward my fellowman
For no weapon that is formed against me
In destruction shall prosper
And every tongue that is raised against me
On judgment day He shall show to be in the wrong
I walk alone and I fear no evil
My faith remains strong

Sabas Whittaker 2000

IN SEARCH OF
(BREAKING AWAY)

Is it love
is it devotion, concern or is it being
So obsessed to lose oneself.

Submerge
Everlasting tolerated frustrations
countless breach of emotional pain
Is it a lust is it a craving
Or a glutton for punishment easily became

Addiction clinked
dominance an uncontrollable link to a fantasy
Awaited need of an ignored self
like a barnacles stuck to an old freighter's haul

Consummated absorption, desire more out of life.
Lead thyself by the hand to the old shipyard
and sandblast thy soul to freedom
Repossess command-
After all, it's just your own life.

Sabas © 1998

RIDING THE WAVES

I was merely a passenger
Luther King and Ghandy's Soul were at the helm
You've work hard at trying to make me whimper
but my spirit remain strong.

Folks around us awaited to see a bloodshed
my courage still focus on a journey long and hard.

When you cursed at me I prayed
While you stumbled the angels kept me afloat
Vigorously you swung your sword at my heart
but the almighty healed my wounds
I submerged deep my faith
Into the arts
The art of living well.

When you drank the devil's soup
intoxicated you spilled venom
in preparation of an attack upon my soul.

I retreated in solitude to find the beauty in His work
I was not alone, God was always by my side.
He anointed my soul and sent angels as my guide.

When you cursed aloud, I remain in silence
When you swung your sword, I prayed for strength
Not a strength to fight, rather that of tolerance to endure.

Now you've fallen, I stand, I deliver
Lessons learned of peace, joy and melodious harmony
But your tears have yet to end.
Wrapped in your blanket of sorrows
and confusions as you are

I've soared to the highest on a tapestry of gold
as I emerged triumphantly in laughter
I pray that God may bless
and help you find your way thereafter.

Sabas Whittaker © 98

UXOR PERFIDIA

A flash of fireworks beneath the skies
A kiss stolen, a new love now born
yet unnoticed by everyone who celebrates

Pain carried within thy heart
anguish now dispersed.
Communicate - To thine neighbors give
a charm, share a smile.

Rejoice - Could I?
For you're now far away from the bitches twisted mind
and destructive fisted hands.

Stand still at a distance
Give an ever-on glance as she crumbles
Perhaps cuddled into miseries frigid bosom
Alas long cry the suckling wolf.

A kiss good bye.
Eyes wide open as if in search for a vessel
afloat on the high seas.

Burdens now unsaddle
unsatisfied orgasm brought about by means of angry sex
satisfactions turned into demands
Beneath the skies lay turmoil
Now no one celebrates.

Sabas Whittaker © 98

THE DEATH AND RESURRECTION OF A SELF ESTEEM

The door resounded with a loud slam
I heard the wild cry, the shout, the curse
Now terrified.
I retreated into stillness.
I walked away didn't even said goodbye.

In heavens bosom to seek refuge
amidst the clouds I disappeared
without even looking back.
Then thunder rolled across the sky's
I vanished into quietness
running away from their good-bye's, their empty hugs.

Late into the restless evening
entwined recalled silent discourse among
Utterance rambling of meaningless words
but sharp to pierce one's heart.

Almost too naive to hear
alike scared the heart to feel the pain.
I laid too long staring through the dark.
Accustomed to such became.

Day by day.
Year by year then passed by

new gathered strength
new confidence to finally shake their hands
in a long and everlasting goodbye.

Sabas Whittaker © 98

I NEVER KNEW HOW MUCH LOVE HURT

I'm in love and I'm feeling good,
though it hurts.
Should I now let you go,
or should I just let my heart and love flow.

If a friend had told me yesterday
this is what I'd been going through
I would've said no way, never not because of you.

It's that kind of love that makes one act like a fool.
You've played the game, sat by the phone
several un-accepted calls and you lose
respect for all the laws and rules.

I am blue and I'm feeling down
soon to be up.
I will come around.

Am just trying to recover from this storm
to maybe live and love again someday
Though I don't believe it'll be with you,
cause I want to feel brand new.

Sabas Whittaker © 1991

WITHOUT A WARNING

Just to think that once I love
just to think how much I cared
Good times and great laughter
once shared.

Your love meant everything in my life
t'was the link which kept it together.
My love meant everything in your life
you said, t'was the reason for your existence.

Naively in love I sat around,
I didn't let you down.
Didn't try to broke your heart,
didn't I brought you pain, nor stormy weather.
without even a warning
you've sat out to find yourself a brand new fella.

Sabas Whittaker © 92

THOUGHT IT WAS LOVE

In my being you searched for the rock,
not for my inner strength, nor kindness.
Glitter of a diamond buried in the rough within.

In your body, soul and spirit I tried to find calm waters,
smooth sailing of a vessel in distrust.
Tormented life.
Tempest, ship in the midst of a long lost night.

        Sabas H. Whittaker © 1997

SCENT OF A LOST LOVE

Rancid fragrance
acerbic heart on a down trodden journey,
dulcet osculation.
Revitalized salty seep trickling down our bodies,
realm of agape and filial.
Why did eros ruled?

Dark hidden places where we once met,
burning beds of passion laid motionless in a valley
of innocence lost for ever to a foolish past.

Dreams of mutuality hereafter turned to lies.
Shattered beings dwelling under one roof,
alike candles struggling to remain lit in the rain.

Rancid fragrance,
acerbic hearths journeying throughout life.

Sabas H. Whittaker © 1997

I REMEMBER YOU.
DO YOU REMEMBER ME?

Remember when we walked together
for many, many miles holding hands.
Without the thought of feeling scared and lonely.

While walking on the beach
our footprints disappeared in the sand.
When my song was your song
and your heart beat was my heart beat
as our hearts blended together in a rhythm of love.
Two lovers lips merged for a long, long kiss.

Remember when we walked together
holding hands with a smile.
when our lips joined
and we became one living soul
As our bodies turned into a joyful waterfall

But now that you're so far away
and our song are not the same any more
now your footprints alike that sand
are being washed by other waters.

You're not mine
and I am not yours anymore,
now our song is not the same anymore.
Maybe someday our song and heart beat

will again be the same.
As our lips merge together for an everlasting kiss

Sabas Whittaker © 1991.

I HAVE LOST YOUR LOVE

Now our love is as feeble
as the dimness of a flickering lamp,
whose oil is at it's furthest
and slowly burns its last.

You once shined bright upon my soul,
filling my heart with glory, happiness and joy.
Our love was alike two fragile butterflies,
redundantly flying together,
enchanted by perfume of roses;
hence attracted to each other
like the seas attracts the shores.

You pushed away my love,
as if the wind inflated your sails
which set your ship to navigate
on to some unknown ocean.

Oh such sadness, emptiness
now burdens my heart,
since you pulled up your anchor
which rooted up my courage to navigate.

Today I've learned
you dropped that anchor
in a distant harbor,
and I have lost your love.

Sabas H. Whittaker © 1991

FORBIDDEN LOVE

My heart knew you were not mine
and that your love belonged to another.
T'was on that lonesome night
when I felt your heart beat...
though we'd spent some time together.

In a sailors dream
you landed upon my vessel.
With satin, wine and roses
you brought into my life a new sunshine.
After the storm, alike a seagull you flew away in time.

How can I ever forget you,
when you are the reason of my existence?
How could have I ever loved you,
when your heart belonged elsewhere?

Loneliness, forgetfulness, destruction.
I must forget you, before I destroy my life...
to which God knows you have no right.

Sabas H. Whittaker © 1991

IS IT A REBOUND?

Winds whistling through a window
where a restless soul lays asleep.
Briskly awakened by the dreams of a lost heart,
As if pricked by a thorn off a dried rose stem.

Fidelity, cardinal devotion
linked to an aura now dimmed.
Ardor silenced quietly throughout the night.
Journey of sunsets traded in.

Uncertainties
plunged thyself into a stormy life.
Or free to set sail in pursuit of the unknown
Like a scream echoing in the dark
I flourished and to light
my senses became

Sabas Whittaker © 1997

NIGHTMARE ON LOVE STREET

Winds whistling through a window pane
inside a restless soul lays asleep.
Briskly awakened by the dreams of a lost heart
as if being pricked by a thorn broken
off of a dried rose stem.

Fidelity, cardinal devotion
linked to an aura now dimmed.
Ardor silenced quietly throughout the night.
Journeyofsunsetstradedin.

Uncertainties
plunged thyself into a stormy life.
Be free to set a sail in pursuit of a long overdue
Happiness, joy and laughter
Like a scream echoing throughout the dark.
There is an end
I've seen the light of courage.
   I've broken away from the chains of pain
And now I move on

Goodbye selfishness, hello happiness
Now I walk on by bout my business
Big smile on my face

Sabas Whittaker © 2000

LYRICS

A SONG TO A SINGLE WOMAN.

(Blues)

1>To this handsome gent this woman was his wife
Picked like a flower in the prime of her life.

Reminiscence of times gone by just like a rose who stem has now dried, a single woman lives her lonely life inside.

Tears of sorrow, tears of pain; searching through her soul in vain.
Tears of sorrow, tears of pain the single woman live day by day.

2> Tears like pearls running down her face as she cries again just to soothe her fears.
Rain drops that look like pearls motionless as she stands,
with an unquestionable fantasy of her long lost man.

Like a bird she must fly raising her wings to wipe the tears from her eyes. Alone she flies again to fight all of her fears. A single woman lives a lonely life inside.

B> Tears of sorrow, tears of pain searching through her soul in vain.
Tears of sorrow tears of pain the single woman live day by day.

A SONG TO A SINGLE WOMAN.

(Country)

Tears like pearls run down her face, as she cries again to soothe her fears.
Tears of sorrow, tears of pain searching through her soul for answers Desolate heart yearning in vain.

Reminiscent of times gone by picked like a flower who stem has now dried.

The single woman cries in desperation, while no one is there; her friends don't try to understand her situation.

With her tear drops like pearls motionless she stands.
Unquestionably fantasizing about her long ago man.

To some unknown gent she once was wife, youth picked like a fruit
in the prime of her life.

Steer straight at her face. Are they pearls, or are they tears?
A bird that once flew, whose broken wings once repaired, will raise those wings and wipe her tears, as she flies again to fight her fears.

Like a vessel that once glided across the oceans,

she'll leave this old port and set her sail;
due for peace she cannot fail. She's due for peace and she will not fail.
She is due for peace and she cannot fail.

Sabas Whittaker © 1991

LOVE COULD FIND US.

Blues

Please let me tell you war is not the solution to peace.
Men seek self fulfillment only to end up with travails and grief.

Tear down the gates, remove the walls; dissolve the laws that chain
 us all.
And let mankind for once stand tall with one voice let us be strong.

      C> Love could find us and we could find love.

Why does the rain still fall and the sun still shines, despite of all
 the abuse upon our Earth?
just think how beautiful this world could be with one voice, one
 love, one harmony.

Tear down the gates, remove the walls dissolve the laws that chain
 us all, and let mankind for once stand tall.
With one voice let us be strong.

C_ Love could find us and we could find love.
If love could find us and we could find love.
Love could find us and we could find love.
Yes we could, yes we could find love.

                                      Sabas Whittaker © 1991

TRIBUTE TO A VIETNAM VET.

<Reggae>

It's easier, God knows it's easier.
In the summer, to live on the streets.
The weather is warmer, the daylight last longer,
they're a few more giving faces,
or I can sleep on the beach.

In winter time, there's a shelter curfew line
As the temp bitterly tumbles and I don't have a dime.

During summer time the pressure eases
I'm still walking down main street
carrying my dreams in fragmented pieces.

The competition for beds are tough
with no one to talk to, I got no one to trust.
Starring at the shadows dancing on the wall
I tried reassuring my self I'm no longer at war.

Remembering war time buddies
as we once fought through the night.
while probing through your garbage
to look for a bite.

Sabas Whittaker © 1994

TRIBUTE TO A ROLE MODEL.

He watched the days go by as slow as winter,
his heart beat was as loud as thunder.
Behind steel bars he prayed and wonder
About the equal rights and justice of his people
once yanked from yonder.

Yet to those attempting to trash his dreams,
his freedom, and his soul he showed no danger.
Dreams washed away like the sea washes the shore,
freedom blown away like leaves in the fall
after transposing into their foliage colors
But even the bitter winter cold,
still failed to freeze his soul.

Although many attempts to tear him apart,
with gospel and truth he won their hearts.
A proper route of life he helped us chart
and to those born during a morality vacation
he gave his heart.

Sabas Whittaker © 1991

MY REVIVAL.

Song (Gospel) .

Amidst our harmony (Exist a revival)
So forceful, as a storm (Exist a revival)
Lightening cannot strike it down. (Exist a revival)
Strong winds can't blow it away. (Exist a revival)

1> There's a deep settled peace in my soul.
Living where, the healing waters flow.

2> There's a deep settled peace, in my soul.
Living where, the healing waters flow.
{There's a deep settled peace, within my soul}
{Revive me revive my soul.}

Hatred and anger can't stand in it's way. (Exist a revival)
Joy, peace and happiness. (Exist a revival)
Fire can't consumed nor burn it away. (Exist a revival)

Sabas Whittaker © 1993

A COMMUNICATION WITH LIFE

Early in August,
when the steeples are steep.
Silver deep dreams that you know you can't reach.

But you tried, but you tried.

The graveyards that mellowed,
on such a long time ago;
with wrought iron fences to block out the show.

As you tried, as you tried.

Iron for rich ones,
they rust when they're old.
Oh poor gents thought,
they were buried in gold.

We must try, we should try.

There are no ships leaving,
this breathless old shore.
You must wait till you're older,
and bore to the core.

So, powder up people.
Don't rub talk on your minds,

you must still keep on praying;
to the Good Lord divine.

You must try, you must try.
you have to try, you must try
and don't give up.

Sabas H. Whittaker © 1992

YOU SEND YOUR SON TO SET US FREE

You send your son to set us free,
so we may live in harmony
You send your son to free the world
to free all man, woman, boys and girls.

Lord thank you Lord for all the good you've done.
We thank you Lord for sending such holy one

You send your son to set us free,
so we may live eternally.
You send your son to free us all
He poured his love and died to heal this world

Lord thank you Lord for all the good you've done.
Good Lord, we thank you oh Lord for sending your only son

Thank you Lord for all the good you've.
Thank you Lord, for sending such holy one

You've give us your love
you sent us your son
you give us your love
you give me your love

Sabas H. Whittaker © 1991 (ASCAP)

TRIBUTE TO A HOMELESS VIETNAM VET.

It's easier,
God knows it's easier
in the summer to live on the streets.

The weather is warmer,
the daylight last longer;
there are a few more friendly faces
and I could sleep on the beach.

    chorus (rep)
In winter time, there's a shelter curfew line;
as the temp. bitterly tumbles
and I don't have a dime.

During summer time, the pressure eases.
As I'm walking down main street,
I see my dreams into fragmented pieces.

    Chorus
In winter time,
there's a shelter curfew mind;
when the temp. bitterly tumbles
I can't even bum a dime.

The competition for beds are though,
I got no one to turn to and I got no one to trust.

Staring at the shadows, as they walk through the walls;
I'm reassuring myself that we are no longer at war.

   Chorus (repeat)
In winter time, there is a shelter curfew line,
when the snow bitterly tumbles
and I don't have a dime.

Remembering wartime buddies,
how we fought throughout the nights,
while picking threw your garbage,
trying to find a bite.

   Chorus
In winter time,
there are shelter curfew minds;
when the temp. bitterly tumbles
and I don't have a dime.

   Song composed by Sabas Whittaker. Reggae and Country style © 1991 (ASCAP)

ALONE

In the winter there's no shelter.
No place to go, no food to eat.
No one to talk too,
no one to trust for my need.

I'm just a shadow in the night,
just to face tomorrow.
I'm just a shadow in the night,
someone who must; face tomorrow: Alone.

To face tomorrow: Alone.
To face tomorrow: Alone.
To face tomorrow: Alone.

In the summer the pressure eases,
but the heat tears me apart.
I still have a problem,
that is threading my soul and heart.

Wearing this coat sure is heavy,
on a cold windy day.
Without my coat I'll be unhappy,
walking around on a cold ground each day.

I'm just a shadow in the night,
just to face tomorrow.
I'm just a shadow in the night;
of someone who must face tomorrow: Alone.

To face tomorrow: Alone.
To face tomorrow: Alone.
To face tomorrow: Alone.
To face tomorrow.

Sabas H. Whittaker © 1991

DON'T LOOK DOWN ON YOUR BROTHER

(Song)

There's a girl drifting down main street
and in her arms she has a child.
She has no place to go, or stay.
She has not even eaten today.

I saw an old man walking down my street,
no winter gear, ragged shoes on his feet.
The crowds just pass him by, and he.
Just walks and he sighs.

There are many of us out there,
society just don't care.
There are many of us out there,
but my neighbors frown and stare.

Don't Look Down.
Don't look down on your brother.
Don't Look Down.
Don't look down on your brother.
Don't Look Down.
Don't look down on your brother, (if you're not going to pick him
   up).

I paused and asked him where he slept,

and he pointed and showed a highway bridge.
He said he once looked and felt like me,
with a home and job, and some friends.

I know a family of four, that once lived next door.
A fire came, now they're out in the rain.
That girl and child, they could not afford the high rent,
now she walks around crying every day.

There are many of us out there,
society just don't care.
There are many of us out there,
but my neighbors frown and stare.

Don't look down on your brother.
Don't look down on your brother.

Sabas H. Whittaker © 1991

A SONG TO OUR CREATOR

Come and sing with exaltation
let us praise our Lord and rejoice
and once in his congregation
sing with triumphant voice

You know that at God's right hand
you could be in glory seated
once Hell on Earth is defeated
Christ victory will command

Since Christ our Lord is living
no more young men shall die
through old fashion gospel teaching
they must rise to him on high

though sinners we maybe
and to our graves be taken
our sins to light shall awaken
we should live in harmony

Come on and sing
come and sing with exaltation
let us praise our God and rejoice
come on and sing

Christ is the only foundation
some builders do reject
but he for my salvation

he is precious and elect
He is the corner stone
on which this church was founded
and so marvelous it sounded
it's the work of my God alone

    Written composed words and Music by Sabas H. Whittaker ©
1992

SPIRITUALS

HYPOCRISY

Rocky path below his naked feet
Sounds of crushed stones heard on long winding streets.
Whisper, gossip in the name of your trusted friend.

Head for home on a solitary journey through life
Live as you dream, alone.

Hypocrisy is the main ingredient
with which vice relishes our virtues.

Putrid odor trying to find reason
Uneven explanation to the why
man act the way they do.

Sabas © 1998

HOW GREAT THOU ART

As thine are so great
spirits collide with one another
as sole emptiness reign within thy soul.

Brag thine self boastfully
how great thou are.
The size of thine palace clamor in utterance
Thy need not forget to mention
the glitter on thine gold fixtures.

For I and only I
remains atop of those around me
I am the self proclaimed best of best's.

As thine are thou great
your spirit has match no other.

Failed reincarnation
of a poor and foolish soul
who still remains adrift in the yonder.

Sabas © 1998

KNOCK, KNOCK KNOCKING ON HEAVENS DOOR

Utopia
A failed dream you tried to reach
with a purchase a donation a makeup kit
an empty song a ritual dance

A shuffle during an offering
tidings given freely
ignored spiritual surrender

Clamor
Religious conviction of a boasted
non existent foundation
Still you knock at Heavens gate.

Insisting you' must be let in
tough your spirit remains at bay
but you've been though you can buy your way in.

Powder up
Wear your best fragrance
A Sunday hat with matching garments
Does this tie go with the suit
while you tote around the biggest book money can buy

Is it a black church?
Or is it a white church?

Tell me how you planned to enter into his presence
What banner would you chose to enter his gate
What coat of arms adorned your spiritual being

Your maid's child still in badly need of health care
a mother who still awaits the long overdue raise promised
Did you stop to give the beggar a dime, a coffee, a donut
or did you stumble as you upped your pace
Be sure to be seeing by all the brothers
as you dropped the $ 100. 00 bill into the plate

Utopian dreams you've tried to reach
with a selfish prayer invoked each day
Is it for your benefit or that of your fellowman

The harmony in your a song ought to be communal
A motion in your ritual dance is to be shared by all

                                    Sabas © 1998

ABSTRACT

Were you chosen to dissect my life I asked
Interviews analysis and question about
common stories we all drag behind which ought to be told
Instead in silence wondered hold
As if to tell ourselves that we cannot change what's already unfold

We have no impact on what will be the outcome of facts already given, reality that's based on perception neither truth, nor intuition. But rather ill treated and maladapted mindset of advise given by the selfish.
Just because jealousy perhaps I wonder

As I stepped into the light t'was the light of reason
Not that which makes us such an overnight success
I've stood in dress rehearsal for many of years
Bare feet empty stomach hopeless not a smile but tears and came face to face with fears to overcome battles lost
Thus the cost paid was high hence to succeed not just survive

Some people will ask why are you in such high position
Why not I then asked We've all been given the same opportunity some perhaps even more thus quantity isn't the main To follow our dream and follow our purpose in life
Alike a salmon we're born to swim upstream, but life is difficult and realizing it's difficult, it'll remain
Though foolish empty and selfish souls will choose to live a lie and eventually die in vain merely to feed an illusion and follow a crowd unable to show their gain

Will you now stand tall and proud will you follow your heart.
   Will you have the courage to answer His call?
You can't find God in a bottle or battle your demons with another
   vice. He's going to find you if you live an upright you'd be led
   by the Spirit
Learn to focus the true meaning of your life
Healed from within and all doubt will disappear to a happy way of
   living you will no longer fear

Temptations always lurk in the shadows to challenge
your faith to fight for what you believe in when you're led by the
   spirit. You cannot conceive conceding A battle already won.
   The Son of God, the Holy Spirit, mindfulness and altruism
   are to remain the chosen way of life.

AWARENESS

Comprehend the water
Comprehend the air
Comprehend how God
Will always be there
Watching, waiting, nurturing and protecting while we're stubbornly neglecting

Does a fish Comprehend water
Does a bird Comprehend the air
Does a man Comprehend God Or simply expects him to always be there

Pray for Strength And God will perhaps give you difficulties to make you strong
Pray for Wisdom And God will give you problems to solve.
Pray for Prosperity And God will give you brain and brawn to work harder
Pray for Courage And God will give you dangers to overcome.

COMPREHENSION
AWARENESS
MINDFULNESS

NO NEED TO DISSOLVE A FETUS (IF I JUST LISTEN AND FOLLOW THEIR ADVICE)

Thirst for a child unquenched tortured and troubled couples paradise
Wait the stork do delivers newer baby's in your world, but wait for your time
Desire closed and surrender day to night rejoice to inner light thy strength

Wants fulfilled my vessel prepared still I thirst for the river not dried
Love of an innocence slowly to arrive thus fast passed by
Child born to a life on a long bent curve and winding roads trapped in a bubble for ever immune to a place in time which bast in ambivalent mood thus cry

Life proven false essence of fragrant love ignited by teenage passion and twisted hormonal flames yet luminous and thus mistaken for self esteem hence drawn on rapturous self claim.

From the deep perpetual wells so long a go dried yet occasionally filled during precise summer storms as incessant burst glow his whistling beacons her
to believe she's wrapped in the tender warmth of night, As she climbs through the window in disguise.

Rinsed through cleansing river of dreams a parent worst nightmare
by which she caries her failed inductment gain into the life long hall of fame
Between dreams caught among turbulent waves imprisoning heated gossip and lazy whispers of rundown neighborhoods in which she dwells. The grand marshal of his self proclaimed parade she will and still remains.

Reduced to the nothingness abound aberrant life now linked by the arms
of an over weight pushing fat harboring though still a teenager himself
Her lover and their four malnourished growing fast in mind and street wise wondering why where they were ever brought here.

Balls of funk driving through fuzzy circles and marching casual parades
Climbing unknown paths fulfilling with laughter the ego's of his homeboys wearing shorts bellow their ankles and untied tennis shoes. No belts just trying showoff their undies inch by inch sarcastically displaying favorite designer brand label. As they copy styles of convicts who's lives they've grown to envy

To the daughter who quit school and now stands in line awaiting a monthly ration of gobament cheese a wic voucher and food stamps. Her burden twice heavier moist air no longer dry to breath the consistent and carved ordained bickering she'd left behind on deaf ears everlastingly inundated in lost childhood tears

T'was her mom and dad who failed to give the good-old fashion advice now etched in a moment long after the fire the piece of pie carved for herself still lingers on as it slowly burns reminders in sadly regretful daily hints.

Painfully hidden behind colors to commit crimes upon the weak yet willing to disguise their assault under the banner and sanctity of culture

My sweet child if I fall in battle please don't just quit to chase the dream

Raise that flag and lead our courageous troop.

CARDINAL
(A WELL OILED HINGE)

Alike the artist who seek the beauty within his paintings
I try to find wisdom in my pathway throughout life
in a world where physical appearances are valued
and inner spirits and morals ignored.
Selfishness remains our main drive.
A sole purpose in life
to succeed at any cause we're taught

Alike a Hitler's fallacy in his search for an Arian race
we stand no better today
Still we remain slaves to the aesthetics
of outer appearances in the name of fashion.
History has thought us nothing,
nothing we have learned from our past.
Billions of bones laid forgotten in the dust.

Listen
Hear the sound of the gong
follow carefully the sound of the bell
observe where it leads your life

Who's eyes are bluer, who's boobs are bigger.
Who's hair is blondest, longest, thickest
Who has the highest Afro, the thinner, thicker lips.
And who's skin is of a lighter, or darker shade.

Listen.
Hear the madness
Discern the difference between vice and virtue
A life ought to be lived as an art
I practiced the art of living well.

                                                  Sabas © 1998

SEASIDE VISION

I stand atop the dunes of sand
and gaze at the sea below
To watch it's changing moods and wrath
its natures picture show.

Far out where my eyes can barely see
the white caps start to form
They line up just like soldiers and
come marching, marching home.

When the stormy seas take hold, and
the waves mount high with power
they crash upon the sandy shores
like volleys of cannon fire.

But morning breezes soothes the waves
to a calm and gentle roll,
and they change their stately white caps
for layers of peaceful foam.

I see the waves from day to day
in thoughts and memories
and think of how they carried me
through life's calm and stormy seas.

Sabas Whittaker

A FATHER'S DREAMS, PRAYERS AND WISHES (CONSOLATION)

A daughter cries
her first love lost
She's daddy's little girl
and help her he must.

For words to cheer he searches... a find for such is in vain
alas he sits beside her attempting to comfort her pain.
He tells her a story of days long gone by
reminiscing his youth where memories lie.

Some boys will hurt you and some make you cry
but daddy will always love you
until the day he dies.

Throughout my search for your mom
I met a lot of girls and made many of them cry
Now somewhere out there, there is a boy
He's out there looking for you
just have a smile on your face whenever he drop's by.

Sabas Whittaker © 1998

A LITTLE PRAYER

My thoughts alike the wind
span time and distance
May God keep you
each and every instance

Be well my friend
be strong
Prayers carried deep within
shall remain until the end.

My thoughts are like the air you breathe
each day I carry you in my heart
and when night falls in my dreams you still remain.

Sabas Whittaker

BETRAYING A CHILD
(THANKS FOR THE LESSON)

Alike a Joseph I found myself
sold, condemned, betrayed and bound
by those most trusted.
My courage kept me alive.

Hands bound in foreign lands
a bruised body, pierced soul and heart broken
were my primary instruments of survival.

You will never amount to nothing
you're destined to become a loser in life...
Those were familiar words heard each day.

Ongoing struggle to erase emotional scars
the anger, the frowns, the curses, brutality endured
still remains.
Scars now used daily as a shield
to protect and fight for the welfare of my fellowman
Their human rights entrusted upon me by a higher being.

But while on the journey, my heart found love.
Now I rejoice, I celebrate.
They failed to break my spirit,
I didn't let them crush nor deflate my soul

They were the grown ups, they were the adults.

I was merely eleven years old.
But my Father helped me find understanding to their anger
As I followed their trail of compassion
and barriers between us, I've now learned to dissolve.

Alike a Joseph I brought them bread
to ease their hunger pains
water and wine to soothe their thirst
and wisdom to heal their warp spirit
Blessed unspoken words carried within.

Your bruises, lashes and thumps
were my pathway to success
and I thank you for the lesson given
My guess is that I've learned them too well.

Sabas Whittaker re-written © 2000

A SONG FOR ALL TO HEAR

I wrote to myself a cheering song
descant which heals my wounds
A him that'll soothe my soul
as I planted the seeds of my tomorrow.

I stepped aside and gaze
They rushed by
Their first greed of purpose sole was that to mount of gold

I stood aside, I saw them fall
their fall was hard and cold
Then walked on by whistling
my hymn thy soul uplifting.

Thus greed remains, but shattered dreams
subsided withered leaf
unscrupulous souls
bent solely on grief.

I wrote a chant to heal my wounds
to soothe my soul, as I harvested the fruits bear.
Descant that eases the pain
while I sow the seeds of love for tomorrow's must and needs

Sabas Whittaker © 1999

COCKTAIL OF VICES

High on a throne of royal estate
that far outshines and supersedes the wealth
Where pretty people play by poker's richest hands
and gorgeous selfish souls shower themselves in pearls and gold.

An exalted Satan rejoices by merit raised
behind the staring wheel he sways
A stupor well provoked
commanded fool applauded.
Cheer him on
Celebrate
Dare him not I beg to later eulogize.

Thus high uplifted beyond hope aspires
celestial virtues rising with glittering attire
more glorious and else dread
he has now squandered money needed
to buy his baby bread.

Role that dice I said!
Deal me a hand.
Deal that same card to me but twice.

Trust thine-selves
they fear no second fate

Sabas Whittaker © 1998

SOLITARY JOURNEY

From thyself to thyneself
the knowledge of what's accomplished
remains unknown to man's blame.
Damn their praises, their gossip and remarks...
the ride is an imbricate and solitary dream.

Premenstrual queen has again failed
to analyze the outline of my personals
So wrongly traced.

Why haggard thyself ... why the intellectual rape
upon such humble being?
Weak...? No, not I.

Speak if you please, shout if you must.
How much do you think this newly built granite wall
cares to hear?
I pray my reach exceeds the grasp and I reap the harvest gain
a foot hold to a well balanced life.
Shouldn't you ask what is that?
Poor soul, who still embraces bails of pain.

To discern both I've learned
What I want and what's my gain
life's profitless greed lead souls
to reap the harvested carcass
bails of sorrows and mountains of pain.

Know then thyself presume not God to be
and look into thine mirror as Narcisus braids thine
hair with strands of self-praise and pity.

Sabas Whittaker © 1998

MY GRANDMA

She spoke with such eloquence.
Words uttered daily as if she lived during
Shakespearean times.
Muttering and expressing differences
commands request and orders
aloud in Queen's English.

Her long and woolly silver hair
in a long braid she carried.
With her long and pointy nose
she smelled from afar when her grand children
were in trouble.

A golden-oak complexion proudly displayed
as a monument to the mixture and diversity of cultures
flowing through her veins.
Part Jewish, part East Indian, part Scottish and part Black.

Alike a rainbow she embraced equality embodied
and spelled out among us.
the beauty and importance of being diverse.
Difference ought not to exist in a lighter or darker shade.
But in the morals one propagates.

Oh grandma... how I long for thine hugs, kisses
and words. Oh the scowling words.

Woe be unto you.

Her favorite words uttered in that sharp Elizabethan thong.
Which made us feel as if she were a living and walking
Shakespearean drama.

When she reprimanded us
I rather received lashes than to hear her powerful voice.
That's how much I loved and respect my grandma.

Sabas Whittaker © 1998

LIFE'S STILL AN ART.

From the ghettos of Central America,
while still holding on to a Honduran garbage can.
The tender age was eleven,
the stride to Costa Rica,
the dreams to become a productive man.

Ventured into unknown and remote lands,
a journey would then began.
Meager in physical appearance,
pigment of a skin to which many failed to grant their trust.

Unparalleled strong will and dreams to fulfill a thirst, and soothe hunger for freedom on a journey that was almost lost in a third world's dust.
Left alone into vast ocean, a drift, Satan's at the helm. Angels to the rescue.

Where is that friend, extend a hand.
Sole purpose of a goal,
yearned altruistic belief.
Prayers powerfully flowing from a bed ridden mother's mouth to her boy, a cross distant oceans; encouraging as they reach.

Prayers that during long travels through foreign lands to a weary and high spirited soul, His gospel brought relief.

Thus destined to follow a dream,
goals, a struggle for spiritual growth.

Many encountered, many believed;
some even offered a free meal.
Hence without the sweat off his brow,
why such sweet deal.

Miles away laid a sick mother, grave afflictions burdened senses,
withered I am no more.
Anent a procreator, sole emptiness.
Heart fill joy, rest steadfast at peace.

Sabas H. Whittaker © 1991

MAY PEACE PREVAIL ON EARTH (SONG)

Chorus
Away from each other we stand, far from one another as men.
Foreign to each-other we stand, strangers to one an other as men.

To the soldier who strongly grasp his weapon to fight in foreign land. To the friend who uses cruel words to doom his fellow man, and to the son who still rebels in anger and against his parents' love stands.

Far from each other we stand, away from one another as men.
Foreign to each other we stand, far from one another as men.

Please let me tell you, war is not a solution for peace, mankind skirmish for self fulfillment and graft; only to end up with travails and grief.

Now, just put your heart to search, look around and ask yourselves
Why do flowers in our gardens still grow in such lucid colors? Why does the rain still fall and the sun continuously shines, despite of the abuse imposed upon our planet earth?

Why do trees still bear edible fruits and oceans recover to share their harvest, after being smeared with foreign refuse?

May peace prevail on earth.
To the husband whose heart spills out abuse and to the young

anesthetized through such drug use.
The children implored that you restrain your selfishness that you divert your sadness into laughter, shift your frown into a smile and let them know there is love.

May peace prevail on earth. As you closed your eyes and visualize how beautiful the world would be without borders to cross, and daily struggles for unearned glories.

As world leaders paused and foresee all of this great love. Please voice your story, because there is love.

Tear down the gates, remove the walls, dissolve the laws that chain us all and let mankind for once stand tall.

Hence as foreigners we motionless stand, be vocal, ask your brothers, ask your neighbors, your sisters.
Yellow, brown, black, or white to step forth to hold your hand.
And with one voice, one love, one harmony let's shout, let's sing.
Thank God almighty for giving us his love May peace prevail on earth. Again we sing, Tear down the gates, remove the walls, dissolve the laws that chain us all and let mankind for once stand tall. May peace prevail, may peace prevail, May peace prevail on earth.

© 1995 Sabas Whittaker

THE ART OF CARING

One God to follow yet so many creeds.
One path in life that should not wind
even if we have mastered the art of being kind.

Sabas H. Whittaker © 94

REVOLUTION FOR THY PEOPLE. WHOM?

An odor still remains on the plantation.
A mixture of blooded bodies, sugar cane, bananas
and cotton gin.

Palm trees replaced by crosses,
beneath them lay shattered bones.
Shallow graves in death-rattles
daily yearn for peace.

Conniving, sly subordinate rulers,
golden goblets in hand
adorned themselves in glittering
gold and silver sashes.

Aesthetic gleam throughout the palace,
compound laughter of vanished voices
in its passageway.

Hidden seeds of tears
spread throughout the land.
Mounted hatred in layers of pain,
there won't be any rain.

Conniving, sly subordinate rulers
golden goblet in hand.
Telephone, I want to call my banker

put me through operator,
put me through to Switzerland,
I want to contact my Swiss bank.

Sabas Whittaker © 1997

ALONE

In the winter there's no shelter.
No place to go, no food to eat.
No one to talk too,
no one to trust for my need.

I'm just a shadow in the night,
just to face tomorrow.
I'm just a shadow in the night,
someone who must; face tomorrow: Alone.

To face tomorrow: Alone.
To face tomorrow: Alone.
To face tomorrow: Alone.

In the summer the pressure eases,
but the heat tears me apart.
I still have a problem,
that is threading my soul and heart.

Wearing this coat sure is heavy,
on a cold windy day.
Without my coat I'll be unhappy,
walking around on a cold ground each day.

I'm just a shadow in the night,
just to face tomorrow.
I'm just a shadow in the night;
of someone who must face tomorrow: Alone.

To face tomorrow: Alone.
To face tomorrow: Alone.
To face tomorrow: Alone.
To face tomorrow.

                              Sabas H. Whittaker © 1991

DON'T LOOK DOWN ON YOUR BROTHER (SONG)

There's a girl drifting down main street
and in her arms she has a child.
She has no place to go, or stay.
She has not even eaten today.

I saw an old man walking down my street,
no winter gear, ragged shoes on his feet.
The crowds just pass him by, and he.
Just walks and he sighs.

There are many of us out there,
society just don't care.
There are many of us out there,
but my neighbors frown and stare.

Don't Look Down.
Don't look down on your brother.
Don't Look Down.
Don't look down on your brother.
Don't Look Down.
Don't look down on your brother, (if you're not going to pick
  him up).

I paused and asked him where he slept,
and he pointed and showed a highway bridge.
He said he once looked and felt like me,

with a home and job, and some friends.
I know a family of four, that once lived next door.
A fire came, now they're out in the rain.
That girl and child, they could not afford the high rent,
now she walks around crying every day.

There are many of us out there,
society just don't care.
There are many of us out there,
but my neighbors frown and stare.

Don't look down on your brother.
Don't look down on your brother.

Sabas H. Whittaker © 1991

A SONG TO OUR CREATOR

Come and sing with exaltation
let us praise our Lord and rejoice
and once in his congregation
sing with triumphant voice

You know that at God's right hand
you could be in glory seated
once Hell on Earth is defeated
Christ victory will command

Since Christ our Lord is living
no more young men shall die
through old fashion gospel teaching
they must rise to him on high

though sinners we maybe
and to our graves be taken
our sins to light shall awaken
we should live in harmony

Come on and sing
come and sing with exaltation
let us praise our God and rejoice
come on and sing

Christ is the only foundation
some builders do reject
but he for my salvation

he is precious and elect
He is the corner stone
on which this church was founded
and so marvelous it sounded
it's the work of my God alone

    Written composed words and Music by Sabas H. Whittaker © 1992

MY RIVAL

Amidst our harmony exists a rival.
So forceful storm fails to blow it away
and lightening cannot strike it down.

It made you forget the unison of our smiles,
joy gave way to envy and anger,
hatred replaced resistance.

Yet this powerful rival,
still contends on armed grounds.

Now in return I will not hate you,
for you are the very rind
that house my soul.
I will enshrine the good times
that have now passed us by
as I crave their return.

My dear God,
how can this rival exist?
I defended our love
much stronger than the wind
which thunders to blow it away.

And more consumed than fire intent on ashes.
Yet this powerful rival still contends on grounds
so armed with hate.

© 1991 Sabas Whittaker

A COMMUNICATION WITH LIFE

Early in August,
when the steeples are steep.
Silver deep dreams that you know you can't reach.

But you tried, but you tried.

The graveyards that mellowed,
on such a long time ago;
with wrought iron fences to block out the show.

As you tried, as you tried.

Iron for rich ones,
they rust when they're old.
Oh poor gents thought,
they were buried in gold.

We must try, we should try.

There are no ships leaving,
this breathless old shore.
You must wait till you're older,
and bore to the core.

So, powder up people.

Don't rub talk on your minds,
you must still keep on praying;
to the Good Lord divine.

You must try, you must try.
you have to try, you must try
and don't give up.

> Sabas H. Whittaker © 1992

YOU SEND YOUR SON TO SET US FREE

You send your son to set us free,
so we may live in harmony
You send your son to free the world
to free all man, woman, boys and girls.

Lord thank you Lord for all the good you've done.
We thank you Lord for sending such holy one

You send your son to set us free,
so we may live eternally.
You send your son to free us all
He poured his love and died to heal this world

Lord thank you Lord for all the good you've done.
Good Lord, we thank you oh Lord for sending your only son

Thank you Lord for all the good you've.
Thank you Lord, for sending such holy one

You've give us your love
you sent us your son
you give us your love
you give me your love

Sabas H. Whittaker © 1991 (ASCAP)

TRIBUTE TO A HOMELESS VIETNAM VET.

It's easier,
God knows it's easier
in the summer to live on the streets.

The weather is warmer,
the daylight last longer;
there are a few more friendly faces
and I could sleep on the beach.

    chorus (rep)
In winter time, there's a shelter curfew line;
as the temp. bitterly tumbles
and I don't have a dime.

During summer time, the pressure eases.
As I'm walking down main street,
I see my dreams into fragmented pieces.

    Chorus
In winter time,
there's a shelter curfew mind;
when the temp. bitterly tumbles
I can't even bum a dime.

The competition for beds are though,
I got no one to turn to and I got no one to trust.

Staring at the shadows, as they walk through the walls;
I'm reassuring myself that we are no longer at war.

    Chorus (repeat)
In winter time, there is a shelter curfew line,
when the snow bitterly tumbles
and I don't have a dime.

Remembering wartime buddies,
how we fought throughout the nights,
while picking threw your garbage,
trying to find a bite.

    Chorus
In winter time,
there are shelter curfew minds;
when the temp. bitterly tumbles
and I don't have a dime.

    Song composed by Sabas Whittaker. Reggae and Country style
    © 1991 (ASCAP)

LOOKING BACK AS LIFE GOES ON.

The lion cries in silence
throughout the quiet night,
as he sat just looking back
at foot prints of times
that long ago went by

Foot prints that took him out of a jungle
where he once thought to be the king
and placed him into a confused world,
where at every other step he stumbles

Stumbling over life formed blocks
to survive temptations he'd known as a child.
Simply because, he has goal, he carries a cross,
he has a drive to still stand tall.
Pride to keep a dream alive.

To young cubs left behind,
he once told the story
and to a few gentle ones
encountered upon his journey,
he showed them love and self respect.

Hearts in which he will forever live
in harmony, peace and glory.

Sabas H. Whittaker © 1991

WHY THE HATE

When we hate
Hatred builds a wall around us
At first we learn to hate the enemy
Then we hate the neighbor
Then our friends
Then our children
Then our brother sister and parents
And when we have no one else to hate
We began to hate ourselves

My heart and soul remains free
Of hatred toward my fellowman
For no weapon that is formed against me
In destruction shall prosper
And every tongue that is raised against me
On judgement day He shall show to be in the wrong
I walk alone and I fear no evil
My faith remains strong

Sabas Whittaker 2000

TO MY HOMELESS NEIGHBOR

Often times we feel that our burden is too large to carry and with our eyes closed to the world around us, we ignore the pain and suffering of others. Perhaps focusing a bit too much solely on ourselves and never once stopping to wonder about the homeless. How can they endure such and still keep on going bout their business? Who are they? Where did they come from, or what misfortune could've brought such a person to accept living in such ways?

Today is payday and in gratitude to my paycheck I will dedicate these few poems to all who are homeless, been homeless at some point in their lives, or are in danger of losing their jobs, their homes and their way of life. Because we're all one but paycheck from the streets.

Don't Look Down On Your Brother, If You're Not Going To Pick Him Up. (To my homeless brothers and sisters) Poem

There's a girl drifting down main street
and in her arms, she has a child.
She has, no place to go or stay.
She has, not even eaten today.

I saw an old man walking down my street,
no winter gear, just ragged shoes on his feet.
Crowds just pass him by and he just walks and sighs.
Oh yes I've seen the crowds just pass him by,
as he just gazes and sighs.

There are many of us out here,

yet society doesn't care.
There are many of us around,
though my neighbors look and frown.
Yeah, yeah there are many of us out here,
but society just doesn't care.

I paused and ask him where he slept?
He pointed and showed me a highway bridge.

Once I looked, felt and acted like you,
I had a home, a job and good friends too

I know a family who once lived next door,
after a fire came, they ended up in the rain.
That girl and child could not afford high rent,
they both have AIDS. yet once night falls
they will embrace the cold cement

There are many of us out here,
though society chooses not to care.
There are many of us who are falling down,
but for some brothers,
the world doesn't even turn.
Meanwhile my friends now,
shun me and push around.

Our numbers are rising my friends.
So as you pass by, remember me.
Don't turn away, but look and see!
As I am now, one day you too might be.
passerby remember me!
Please don't look down on your brother,
if you're not going to pick him up.

Sabas H. Whittaker © 1991

EITHER YOU, EITHER ME (MY HOMELESS NEIGHBOR)

It's time to line up at the shelter
for a warm meal once again,
or I might just wonder down main street
and see who is the new member of our club my friend.

I once was a family man, who had a mortgage and bills to pay,
but now I am searching through your garbage.
I am just trying to grab a meal today.
I was a working man, who had taxes,
car insurance and medical bills to pay.

My son contracted AIDS.,
I've lost my family and our lovely home.
The bills, they just don't go away.
Now I must crumble through your garbage
hoping to find a meal today.

I had a full time job, I worked a lot of overtime,
but since my heart attack,
I haven't even earned a dime.

We the homeless and Aids. victims,
are simple people of familiar stereo type,
caught up in the midst of your political fight.

Entwined with society runaways and rejects.

And they're some of us who's lives has
traditionally been out of control, due to mental illness,
or drug abuse; which many of our own politician have used.

So, it's time to line up at the shelter
for a warm meal once again,
or I might just wonder down main street
and welcome new members to our club my friend.

Sabas H Whittaker © 1991

DIFFERENT FACES DIFFERENT WAYS (MY HOMELESS NEIGHBOR #2)

All of the good times, all of the joy,
but none of their love went up in smoke.

Raising his hands to the skies,
he cried out, dear God is this a joke?

To him it was the beginning of a long nightmare,
from which he has yet to awaken.
To his family it meant the end of a show,
where the function was over
and the curtains were drawn.

Like a castle built out of playing cards
their life crumbled down.
He now walk the streets from dust, to dawn.
Along with his sick wife and kids,
whom for food and for sleep they yearn.

Sweet faces seen on the streets,
that will never give you a cruel word,
or show you a frown.

Sabas Whittaker © 1991

ALONE

In the winter there's no shelter.
No place to go, no food to eat.
No one to talk too,
no one to trust for my need.

I'm just a shadow in the night,
just to face tomorrow.
I'm just a shadow in the night,
someone who must; face tomorrow: Alone.

To face tomorrow: Alone.
To face tomorrow: Alone.
To face tomorrow: Alone.

In the summer the pressure eases,
but the heat tears me apart.
I still have a problem,
that is threading my soul and heart.

Wearing this coat sure is heavy,
on a cold windy day.
Without my coat I'll be unhappy,
walking around on a cold ground each day.

I'm just a shadow in the night,
just to face tomorrow.
I'm just a shadow in the night;
of someone who must face tomorrow: Alone.

o face tomorrow: Alone.
To face tomorrow: Alone.
To face tomorrow: Alone.
To face tomorrow.

Sabas H. Whittaker © 1991

TRIBUTE TO A ROLE MODEL

He watched the days go by as slow as winter,
his heart beat was as loud as thunder.

Behind steel bars he prayed, he wondered,
about the equal rights and justice
of his people once yanked from yonder.

Yet to those attempting to trash his dreams,
his freedom, his soul, he showed no danger.

Dreams that were almost washed away,
like the sea when washes the shore.
Freedom blown away,
alike the leaves during the fall season
after transposing into beautiful colors.
Yet even the bitter winter cold, still
failed to freeze his soul

Although many attempts
to tear him apart, with gospel and truth
he won their hearts.

A proper rout of life he helped us chart
and those born during a morality vacation,
he gave his heart.

Like a shepherd he led his flock
to the realization of un-accomplished dreams.

To freedom, equal rights and justice,
he was a native drive.

Steadfast for non violence he stood affirm
A father, a husband and a son at heart,
who left us behind such instruments of inspirations for peace
this cruel world he then departs.

        Sabas H. Whittaker © 1991

HARVEST

{The Dance of the Locust}

I sowed seeds of hope in the spring
to honor those who have trampled upon my soul,
with hopes of harvesting fruits of harmony and peace in the upcoming fall season.
Journey of a soul in harmony.

Disharmony gave way to thy sails in a storm.
Bend thy knees,
fold thy hands.
Rejoice, thou has created a turmoil.

Blasphemy,
daily you've chosen to use the name of God to justify wrong doings.

Sabas Whittaker © 1997

THE LEGACY OF A BROWN-NOSSER

To he who carelessly laughs
at his neighbors expense
Who never consider non other than himself
but always awaits for someone else to take the fall
meanwhile he reaps the benefits

Fruit of labor
Labor of love
Now run to the boss
you've work hard for many years
mastering the skills of deceit

Sabas © 1998

TRIBUTE TO A ROLE MODEL

He watched the days go by
as slow as winter
his heart beat was as loud as thunder

Behind steel bars he prayed, he wondered,
about the equal rights and justice
of his people once yanked from yonder.

Yet to those attempting to trash his dreams,
his freedom and his soul,
he showed no danger.

Dreams washed away,
like the sea washes the shore.
Freedom blown away,
like leaves during the fall season
after transposing into beautiful colors.
Yet even the bitter winter cold, still
failed to freeze his soul

Although many attempts
to tear him apart, with gospel and truth
he won their hearts.

A proper rout of life he helped us chart
and those born during a morality vacation,
he give his heart.

Like a shepherd he led his flock
toward the realization of un-accomplished dreams.
Freedom, equal rights and justice,
he was a native drive.

A father, a husband and a son at heart,
leaving behind such instruments of inspirations for peace.
This cruel world he then departs.

Sabas H. Whittaker (C 1991)

YES...THERE IS LOVE (MAY PEACE PREVAIL) POEM

To the soldier who strongly grasp his weapon
to fight in foreign land.
To the friend who uses cruel words
to doom his fellow man,
and to the son who still rebels in anger
and against his parents' love stands.

Please let me tell you
war is not the solution for peace...
mankind skirmish for self fulfillment and graft
only to end up with travails and grief.

Just shift your heart to a search.
Look around and ask yourselves?

Why do the flowers in the gardens still grow in such lucid colors?
Why does the rain still fall and the sun continuously shines, despite of the abuse imposed upon our planet?
Why do trees still bear edible fruits and oceans recover to
share their harvest, after they've been smeared with foreign refuse,
If there were no love.

The children implored that you restrain your selfishness
that you divert your sadness into laughter. Shift your frown into a
smile and let them know that there is love.

As world leaders to pause and foresee all of this great love.
Then please voice your story, because there is love.

So tear down the gates. Remove the walls. Dissolve the laws that chain us all and let mankind for once stand tall.

Hence as foreigners to each other we stand. Be vocal, ask your brothers, your neighbors, your sisters. Yellow, brown, black, and white to step forth and hold your hand.

And with one voice, one love, one harmony we'll shout, we'll sing.
Thank God almighty for giving us his love May peace prevail
May peace prevail, May peace prevail on Earth
Again we sing Tear down the gates Remove the walls. Dissolve the laws that chain us all and let mankind for once stand tall.

May peace prevail, may peace prevail, May peace prevail on earth.

Sabas Whittaker © 1991

TRIBUTE TO A ROLE MODEL

He watched the days go by
as slow as winter
his heart beat was as loud as thunder

Behind steel bars he prayed, he wondered,
about the equal rights and justice
of his people once yanked from yonder.

Yet to those attempting to trash his dreams,
his freedom and his soul,
he showed no danger.

Dreams washed away,
like the sea washes the shore.
Freedom blown away,
like leaves during the fall season
after transposing into beautiful colors.
Yet even the bitter winter cold, still
failed to freeze his soul

Although many attempts
to tear him apart, with gospel and truth
he won their hearts.

A proper rout of life he helped us chart
and those born during a morality vacation,
he give his heart.

Like a shepherd he led his flock
toward the realization of un-accomplished dreams.
Freedom, equal rights and justice,
he was a native drive.

A father, a husband and a son at heart,
leaving behind such instruments of inspirations for peace.
This cruel world he then departs.

Sabas H. Whittaker © 1991

NIGHTMARE ON LOVE STREET

Winds whistling through a window pane
inside a restless soul lays asleep.
Briskly awakened by the dreams of a lost heart
as if being pricked by a thorn broken
off of a dried rose stem.

Fidelity, cardinal devotion
linked to an aura now dimmed.
Ardor silenced quietly throughout the night.
Journey of sunsets traded in.

Uncertainties
plunged thyself into a stormy life.
Be free to set a sail in pursuit of a long overdue
Happiness, joy and laughter
Like a scream echoing throughout the dark.
There is an end
I've seen the light of courage.
   I've broken away from the chains of pain
And now I move on

Goodbye selfishness, hello happiness
Now I walk on by bout my business
Big smile on my face

Sabas Whittaker © 2000

A COLLECTION OF SHORT STORIES, STORY LINES AND SYNOPSIS OF SCREEN AND STAGE PLAYS

DIFFERENT FACES DIFFERENT WAYS

Lavorne Williams, a middle age black woman husband was an insurance executive in Connecticut, but after years of marriage and living an upper middle class suburban lifestyle, he is dismissed off the corporate ladder and proceeds to fall through society's cracks. In despair, he turns to alcohol and drugs, and daily began to abuse his wife and children. Lavorne, later becoming homeless with her two young children, however, due to her strong spiritual beliefs and moral ethical standards, she is able to overcome the abuse endured at home, the demeaning existence of life in a shelter, and other seemingly unbearable obstacles. Lavorne, is determined to explore and correct the country's increasingly dysfunctional civility. By rising above it all, she becomes a major figure in
American political history, and an inspiration to all.

This story is about an educated young black woman, who through a string of events ends up on the streets, but fights the odds, the system and ends back up on the top. This story deals with a number of social issues such as homelessness, domestic violence, racism and the abuse one can suffer by the system as it now exists; and how one person through unrelenting effort, can make a change for the better. It's about how she struggled with her two children to overcome obstacles encountered in their day to day lives. However, in herspiritual fight to find the golden mean, she confronts political, social, economical and moral issues afflicting our society. Such struggles lead her to open up the first twenty-four-hour day-care center in the country for working parents. She also founded and organized NACSO, the National Association for

A Color Blind Society and TURBO The Urban Rebirth Organization. She also organized and spearheaded a march on Washington, DC, which challenged the Republican's Parties Contract With America. Such later influenced her to become a candidate for the presidency of the United States of America. Lavorne, later goes on to become the very first woman President of the United States and the very first person of color to hold the highest office in the land.

(This body of work is a 250 page manuscript, written in a standard film format as a television miniseries, or movie of the week and could also be easily adapted to the stage as a dramatic piece, or as a musical. It contains over twenty one original copyrighted songs composed by the author). This manuscript /screen play will also be negotiated for possible publication with Xlibris as a shooting script

Sabas Whittaker Copyright 1993.

xxxxxxxxxxxxxxxxxxxxxxxxxxxxxxxxxxxxxxxxxxxxxxxxxxxxxxxx

MENTAL CRAZE, OR VOGUE.

Salcedo graduated from Harvard University with a master in philosophy, in 1965. Everyone wanted a piece of him. He was angry at the world's injustice and treatment toward our indigent population and also disappointed with America's social injustice toward inner city and Southern blacks and about the countries cleansing of its' underprivileged, by sending those less fortunate to fight and die in Vietnam. His father wanted him to go on to law school and follow in his father's and uncles foot steps, whom were all prominent attorneys and politicians throughout the North East. His mother prayed that he focus on a writing career and Uncle Mike, a Massachusetts legislator pushed politics down his throat, but all he wanted was to be left alone. In the midst of trying to sort out life off campus and decide what he wanted to do in life, he was drafted. Being a philosophy major, he was definitely anti war and he refused to go. Therefore, the week after graduation, he joined the Peace Corps. Salcedo requested he be sent somewhere where he could contribute to the goodness of the world, rather than to its destruction and ended up in Honduras.

While in Honduras, Salcedo dedicated himself to teaching peasant farmers the usage of advance and technological farm equipment's, how to become and remain self sufficient and to collaborate jointly with each other in order to compete with the powerful landowners of the region. He thought them that by using a more collaborative effort, they could easily purchase their own trucks and take their products to the market, rather than having to settle for whatever price the land pirates with tractor trailers offered to pay them. Well, this wouldn't go over too well with the local politicians, especially those involved in corrupted agricultural affairs.

And year after arriving in Honduras, he is accused of being a non Christian Socialist, jailed and is later deported on grounds that he was conspiring with the communist party to undermined the country's democratic agenda.

Upon his return to the States, he walked around preaching in market squares, parks, on beaches and anywhere he could find an ear to listen to him. He preached philosophy, altruism, covenant, social contracts, morality, ethics and insisted that we began putting them to practice in our daily living. He also strongly believed that until there is peace between religions, there could be peace among mankind. Though at the time, the trend in America was organized gospel and tele-evangelist were on the rise. He took on the Catholic church and other religious groups in a series of heated debates and was captured, labeled insane and confined to live indefinitely in a mental institution. Only to realize years, later that the same church and government that had put him away thirty years earlier; had finally awakened to the realization of what he'd preached years earlier, could contribute to world peace. The acceptance of racial diversity, help to end world hunger and pave the way for a harmonious new millennium. Pope John Paul IV's pleads for his release to the US governments on his way back from his visit to Cuba. Supreme Court, also petitioned he be released, Juan Carlos Salcedo is released, all of his books, poems and essays published, and is later embraced by intellectuals world wide and considered the father of XXI century and new age philosophy.

Sabas Whittaker © 1995

SCOPY'S JOURNEY

Kaleidoscope, (Scopy) the unicorn, lived and rode throughout the bowels of the universe with a pack of primitive and prehistoric characters causing destruction. His gang being comprised of two headed snakes, fire spitting dragons, half man - half beast barbarians and a variety other vicious characters. They journeyed through cities and towns destroying everything in their path. After being badly beaten and left for dead in a desert by several members of his own posse, he is rescued by Synderesis, The Father of good, who takes him up to the heavens peaceful palace within the clouds and teaches him to reach magnanimity and to find a new way of life.

Months go by and Scopy, is then sent down from the heavens to teach Glendale Forest dwellers animals how to get along and live in peace with each other. Scopy also teaches them how to apply moral values to their daily way of life. His mission being met with great success, during his journey throughout the North American forest, he is able to create an environmental safe haven, thus preventing the panda's extinction.

Synderesis, pleased with Scopy's good work, upon his return to the palace, he is later sent back to earth on a new mission. The journey. This time landing in a city where discrimination is a daily experience encountered by all citizens and hunger and homelessness was for many a way of life. In his quest to eliminate racism, he struggles to decimate drug abuse, gang violence and the negative ways by which we all live.

Sabas Whittaker © 1993

WHILE I WAS PRAISING THE LORD

Erena comes from a tiny prosperous seaside Jamaican village. She is Reverend Douglas's daughter, minister of the town's only church. The burden she carried, was the fact that she was an ambitious, witty, intelligent, studious and career oriented seventeen year old girl in a small town. Some hated her, few liked her very much. Erena also thought Sunday school, played the piano and sang in her father's church choir. Most young men liked her, but felt intimidated around her, some boys talked about her and gave her a bad name. During high school, she gained a reputation of being too stuck up by the men and women considered her an attention seeking, boyfriend snatching brat; though she didn't have, nor wanted a boyfriend. However, those who understood and liked her, saw her as a child prodigy and a phenomenal blessing in the prosperity of their small community. At times, even they couldn't understand her. In part, due to it being uncommon for a young women to possess such qualities and aspire to such high dreams. This was a set standard throughout the West Indies, often times even for some men.

At a young age, she realized that a young woman couldn't go too far in her hometown, but she didn't settle in defeat. Her mother Paulette, the town's seamstress, sewed for the Mayor's wife, the town's doctor's wife and for several other prominent families from neighboring villages and towns. All her life, she dreamt of attending an Ivy league college in the United States, Canada, or England; her parents ultimate goal, was to grant her such a wish, as a reward for all of her hard work and accomplishments. Her mother's business grew, her father worked his farm and saved for his little Erena's education. However, as near by towns prospered, the Douglas's, house-hold income declined. The town to the West of her village opened a supermarket, therefore, the sale of his corn, coffee and vegetables dropped. The town to the South of them also prospered and opened a mall, which specialized in imported goods and bargains on designer's clothing. Shortly thereafter, even with both parents income combined, it wasn't enough to afford to send their only child away to college in Kingston. Still, all she talked about, was attending a prestigious university abroad and studying the arts.

She kept her head up high and her dreams alive while maintaining her optimistic ideals. From an early age she'd spent countless hours in the local library reading about foreign countries and looking at pictures of colleges and universities in England, the United States and Canada. But as usual each day after school, she'd return home and awake to the reality and the fear that her aspirations would never come to fruition. The answer to her dreams appeared to have arrived one day during the summer, when they receive news that an American, Baptist and Methodist revival was scheduled to be held throughout Jamaica's North coast and that her father's church was chosen as a host church. Over a hundred and eighty ministers and a large number of members of their congregation fly in from Central America, Canada, the United States, Europe and neighboring Caribbean islands to the little prospering towns and sleepy villages that summer. Some of them, bringing their entire family.

Most of the American's stayed in Erena's hometown. Reverend Earl Thompson from Hartford Connecticut, became known as the man to have delivered the best sermon villagers had ever, heard, when he preach about trust and faith. Those were just some of the comments surfacing throughout the rest of towns the following day. He staid at Erena's home for a week, her mother and father proudly played host to him and his family and were honored to have him preaching at their church. But from the moment Reverend Earl Thompson's eyes caught glimpse of Erena, he began acting like the fox in Little Red Ridding Hood. More so, when he learned of her interest in studying abroad. He needed a maid for his pregnant wife and right away he put his plan into effect. He made an offer to her parents, which he knew they wouldn't refuse, deliberately misleading them. Reverend Thompson, assured them that if they allowed Erena to return to the States with them and help his pregnant wife with their other two children a five and a three year old, they would make sure she acquired the education she deserved. Shortly after arriving back in Connecticut, they practically enslaved and worked her half to death. Reverend Thompson, confiscated and read her incoming mail, lie to her about moneys they supposedly were sending back home for her parents and about a college fund which was never started. Erena, becomes depressed and several times rebels, but they simply threatens to write her parents and tell them lies about her. Once, he even threatened to call the Immigration and turn her in for working, while being undocumented in the country. For months Erena worked and tolerated the Thompson's abuse, out of fear and respect for her parents, as she pray her nightmare soon to end. During the few times she is allowed to attend church, she mets Winston, a young man to whom she becomes fond of. Once Reverend Thompson finds out and plots a way to keep her from seeing him. A somewhat naive and pregnant, Mrs. Thompson, continue praising her husband, and promising Erena that, as soon as she delivers, she would start attending school. Nevertheless, after she had the baby, things only gotten worse for Erena, the bulk of dirty diapers became larger and so did the overall house work. The situation also gives Reverend Thompson, the opportunity to be alone for longer periods with Erena. His advances toward her also grows and he eventually he gets his long awaited prize. Erena becomes pregnant by Reverend Thompson, he blames it on Winston and she is kicked out of the Thompson's home. Mrs. Thompson thought it immoral to have a young, pregnant, single girl living under the same roof with a wholesome Christian family. Though no one in town knows its the reverend's child she carries, they casts judgment upon her and even forbids their daughters from speaking to her. Some of the church members suggests sending her back home, others suggested placing her in a home for unwed mother's and letting her put the child up for adoption, but Erena doesn't care for neither of their suggestions. She doesn't want to disrespect her father and mother in such a way, nor does she wants her town folks to feel that she let them down. They would never understand, nor would they believe me (she thought). At first the idea of being place in a home for unwed mothers sounds good, but as the child inside of her grows, so does Erena's maternal love for her baby and same day she is placed in the home, she runs away to New York.

While in New York, she unsuccessfully tries to gain employment during the day, while living on the streets and sleeping in Grand Central Station and shelters at night, until she is taken in by a Colombian family, who takes care of her during the last of her pregnancy. Soon after giving birth, she realizes that there is no way she is going to be able to survive with a child and provide a safe and stable home for it. So, she opts to let the Colombian couple adopt the baby and she takes off to Los Angeles, California in search of a better future.

Twenty four years had gone, Patricia, Erena's baby was getting ready to enter medical school, her adoptive Colombian parents had revealed her biological mother's origin. The quest for Patricia to find her mother takes her on a roller coaster journey, throughout Connecticut, California and the Caribbean. She mets with her living grandparents and other relatives she didn't even knew she had. During her long search, she also meets her mother's first love, Winston. He now owned a private investigations agency and places all his resources into succeeding with their search for Erena. Erena, now married, was a successful film and television producer in Los Angeles. The three latter return to Connecticut to testify in Reverend Earl Thompson's long over due rape trial. Being only one month away from the expiration of the statute of limitation.

Sabas Whittaker © 1995

HURRICANE BABIES
(SHORT STORY)

This story begins on a banana plantation in Honduras, though it might same unique, it's merely another tragedy alike the thousands heard throughout the country since October and November in the aftermath of hurricane Mitch.

Noa, was barely twenty five days old, when he was to sail upon the turbulent waters; alike his namesake in the old testament. Except he did not have an arc in which to braze the storm.

A young matrimony, Samuel and Karina Melendez, and their little son, Noa await and watch as the rain continued to fall, as they had done so many times in the past. They paid little attention to the raising waters on the riverbank. "We were used to it. the floods around here in the Valle de Sula are so frequent that we pay them no mind. When it rains and our homes get flooded, we simply go on top of the roof and await until water levels drop and when we're able to again see the banana plantations, we then that now it's safe enough to climb back down."

But this time it was different. Three days without eating was more than enough for little Noa to find any milk as he suckles on his mother's breast. Without thinking twice about the depth of the water, Samuel, took Noa, placed him into a basin and together with his wife they embarked on a desperate journey to save his life as they floated onto logs drifting down the river bank.

Hector Alfonso Avila, after quick thinking alike one thinks in desperate times, climb down the roof of his home and proceeded to improvise by building a makeshift boat with an inner tube, some rope and a few blankets. He placed his two children in it and him and his wife hanging on to the sides, floated down lake.

The odyssey lasted two hours on the banana farm, now turned into a lake. A place were eight days later, over four hundred families were still trapped on their rooftops and unable to get down.

"The first few days, we were able to eat the meat off of a cow's body that were being dragged by the current." Avila tells us sobbing.

"What have happened to us, is alike a horrible dream; one that we rather soon forget." Added Mr. Francisco Gomez, whom together with his wife and three children had abandoned his home in Arena Blanca.

The Honduran children unknown to the devastation of the tragedy, are alike the rest of children throughout the world. Running around playing half-naked in the high raised waters and laughing in the rain. At times cold during the nights, adhering to the suit of wet clothing they have been wearing for the last four days. Throughout the day they remain the playful, only to fall weary from exhaustion at dusk. Words gushing from their lips in protest "Mother, food please."

"Food, what food? Eat, eat what? When we abandoned our home in search of a safe place, we left everything behind. Now everything is lost. Nor clothes, nor food, we've lost everything. Well, not everything, at least we still have ourselves, thank God" Lamented dona Faustina.

It's a living nighmare, in which thousands of Honduran children have enjoyed in their dreams of a plate of rice and beans, tortillas; some of them have awakened still struggling and forcefully trying to still retain the piece of chicharon between their little fingers.

I remember Betty Lopez, the seventeen year old who gave birth in the canoe which she was being rescued from her over flooded home in barrio El Robles. It was almost miraculously how family members and neighbors shielded and protected her on the dangerous border of the rio Ulua until she was rescued.

I saw them came in droves, alike a human herd of cattle. Scared, shaking and unprotected. All, mostly children. Most of them coming in from the Valle de Sula, such lands being the most fertile in the country probably are going to remain flooded perhaps for months.

Throughout the city of San Pedro Sula, there are over two hundred shelters for the victims of this devastation, but there is still a great need. Specially one with to accommodate these children. In this city we have over fifty thousand homeless children, a large number of them are orphans. They range in all ages from several weeks of age to early teens. (Commented a Honduran Relief nurse as she sobbed). "We must begin to focus our attention to them, they've seen enough."

Their sweet dreams now turned into nightmares, as if they'd abandoned all hope. In Tegucigalpa, there are over ten thousand children tightly packed in like sardines in a shelter. At times, they would revive the horror scenes of torrential rain, wind, water and floods destroying their homes and provoking landslides throughout their neighborhood. The little ones on their parents shoulders, while their oldest siblings held tightly on to mom's squirt tails and dad's pants pockets in the mid's of the wet and cold dark night. As I visit the shelters,

I found human mass upon human mass of dispossessed children. Their little bodies, embracing the cold cement where they laid.

Averaging four to five per family, they collectively occupied their space. And as if forming strands alike human pearls, each finding his little brother, or sister's hand, or his father shoulder, while the littlest of the family suckles upon his mother's breast; perhaps to feel lest fear as they slept.

These stories may perhaps fill pages upon pages, of news print and books in years to come, moreover, I rather it be synthetize in the sad, confused and mistrustful stare found in the eyes of the children. "Mami, here comes another wave and it's dragging away my shoes" Little Carmen cries out night after night, as she relives another nightmare while her mother tries comforting her, both crammed like sardines into a shelter. Her little body lingering due to a long overdue starvation and thirst. Filth heck yeah, there isn't any water for them to shower. "Well, yes. I'll take that back, there is water, tons of it as a matter of fact, but it's the darn cursed water that's good for nothing but to cause more harm." Commented Don Tulio, a farmer from Tibombo. "Though sometimes we are forced to used it, but we must boil it first, however, the kicker is that we have not sufficient dried firewood to spare." Stated Dona Maria, his wife. "It's even worse when we have to used the damn contaminated water to prepare the baby's bottles, I don't care how long we boiled it" Maribell yelled from over in the corner where she sat on the floor breast feeding an infant. I later found out that she'd spent over seven days on a roof top with her two children and seventy others. Here are these little ones and if they'd ever seen a kangaroo, I'm quite sure there were times when they must have envied the young marsupials for their mother's maternal pouch were they would've hidden, to avoid seen such disgrace and destruction and feel no pain, throughout the long and cold dark nights.

But we move on, the young has now learned to pronounce the word huracan (hurricane). Though for them, the significance of such a word is now synonymous with the meaning of being homeless, clotheless, foodless, and thirsting for the lack of water. Losing all your little neighbors, friends and classmates, all yanked away in one crewel night. The story behind those sad days could only be written in the unhappy and heavy hearted stares seen in the eyes of the children. The ones who's yesterday's poverty has been magnified and is now grater, because it is shared with thousands more whom have now joined them on a journey of a tragedy which they've yet to understand, but is rather felt throughout their little innocent bodies.

FOREIGN EXCHANGE

This screenplay is an action-adventure of the mind with a twist. It's a story about a former merchant marine who goes on to become the President of Liberia. After a ten-year war created by the previous administration, he attempts to clean up corruption and reestablish peace. He tries to seek help from his veteran marine buddies, whom he sailed with twenty years earlier. However, they were now living throughout Central America and the United States. With his every move, being carefully monitored by the opposition and only safe way out of the country, reach them and reestablishing contact without being discovered, was to disguise himself in women's clothing and travel abroad by boat. This is the story of three young men from diverse racial, cultural and political backgrounds. Their struggle and courage at sea during their early years and their spirit to conquer bigotry and ignorance encountered on their ship by it's commanding officers. And the development of a brotherhood, which enables them to overcome racial superiority and therefore lead them into romance, adventure and unity on the high seas, while still maintaining their moral values.

It is about three young merchant marines from different countries and cultural backgrounds. How they struggle to get along and overcome their differences, and together accomplish successful careers at sea. How they dealt with the bigotry, ignorance and cruel nature of their ship's captain for almost a year, until on a New Years Eve when their ship caught fire, perishing everyone on board but them. The three were rescued out of the waters two days later by a paramilitary outfit maneuvering around international waters near the coast of Panama and Costa Rica. They joined the outfit and in two years became trained commandos in tactical military warfare. Separated from each other for almost twenty years, now reunited for a cause pledged back in their youth. After being discharged years earlier and deciding upon career changes, one went on to become a social worker, who now worked with Latin American abused and abandoned children in Honduras. The other becomes a cop in New Haven Connecticut, and the third, goes into politics and becomes the leader of his small West African country, but after a ten-year war created by the previous administration, he attempts to clean up corruption and reestablish peace. However, finding himself with both hands tied, he finally decides to seek help from his veteran marine buddies whom he'd sailed with twenty years earlier. They now lived in Central America and the United States. To reestablish contact without being discovered, he must disguise himself as a woman and is smuggled out at night.

This is the story of three young men, their struggle, courage and spirit at sea during their early years. And the development of a brotherhood, which enabled them to aid in the conquering and pacification of a war, ravaged nation and peacefully quell the anger and violence, carried for so long in the hearts and soul of its people. This story deals with romance, adventure, action and unity on the high seas, and shines the light on third world countries political corruption. (This fictional piece is a 135 page manuscript that draw unrelenting facts and brings forth negative stereotypes and real life encounters that American and foreign merchant marines endured on board non American registered vessels. The story also depicts the adventurous life styles of the seventies, prior to the AIDS era).

Sabas Whittaker © 1996

FOREIGN EXCHANGE II

Synopsis

William Gretkal, Demby Lumumba and Hernan Flores, three young merchant marines and newly graduates from merchant marine Academies of three different countries. William Gretkal, age twenty four, born in West Hartford Connecticut and a graduate of the Long Islands Merchant Marine Academy, class of 1975, in Long Island New York. Demby Lumumba, age twenty-three, born in Liberia, West Africa and a graduate of The San Cristobal Academia Maritima, in Milan Italy, also in 1975. And Hernan Flores, a seventeen year old. Though he happened to be the youngest of the three, he was also the most experienced and most qualified. Being born at sea, during one of his mother and father's voyage between The US. Virgin Islands and Honduras, Central America, while his father was employed as a merchant marine officer by Onasis's, Olympia Oil Shipping Company. He'd already spent two and a half years at sea, working with his father a board the Olympia Star as a quarter master and on the S/S Agape, as a cadet on the bridge. While at sea, he studied navigation, Morse code communications, scuba diving and under water welding. And he'd also made time to train as a boatswain, while he concentrated on making enough money to help support his six younger brothers and sisters and pay for his now divorced and terminally ill mothers' medical bills.

Though Hernan, had not yet attended a traditional merchant marine academy, still he possessed the necessary qualifications and training that would've enabled him to become a fine merchant marine officer a board any vessel, no matter the tonnage capacity. It was rooted deep within, he'd came from a long line of black Jack's, traced back to the mid XVIII century. Hernan had also just return from the Base Naval de Honduras, a   military and merchant marine officers training academy located on the north coast of Honduras. There he'd completed six grueling months of intense training in navigation, lifeboat commanding patrol and large cruise carriers' deck management. He also now held a full-fledged officer's license in hand and had been promised a job as an officer with the company. His father, now retired had also worked for the same company as a chief officer. Following in his father's footstep, he was ready to board the S/S Themos, as a third officer; at least that's what he thought. He had successfully performed in the past, as an officer for the Olympia Line and aboard a couple of United Fruit Company ships as well. He'd learn to carry out his duties and responsibilities in emergency situations at sea, alike any other officer and was as confident, and able to perform his duties on the bridge and deck if only given the chance to. Demby, Hernan and William, arrived early in the afternoon on separate flights to the Saint Joseph Airport. They met shortly after arriving in New Orleans, while awaiting the ship's agent on the airport to arrange their transportation and health clearance, before boarding the 56, 000 ton, Greek oil tanker, the S\S Themos.

Sabas Whittaker © 1994

A FAMILY REUNION AT THE RALLY

For almost three years Linnette and Clarence work side by side, tending geriatric patients. They worked during the same hour shifts, in a state run nursing home before discovering that they were actually brother and sister. The two made small talk about the weather, their patients, medications and about labor-management, but never picked up on the fact that they were siblings separated as children. It took a curious coworker to make the connection after hearing two similar stories from Linnette, now 30 and Clarence, 31. When Clarence, tells his coworker, Issac Shields that he'd been abandoned by his mother and sister as a child and several months later, Linnette tells Issac almost the same story in reverse. When she tells him that she had a brother she hadn't seen in almost thirty years. The pair was split apart when their mother Beverly, took off with Linnette then only six months old, leaving Clarence behind with his father Edward, who lived in Hartford Connecticut. Beverly had moved out of the state and taken Linnette to live with her mother in Forth Lauderdale, Florida. Edward, who wasn't Linnette's father, chose not to pursue her and staid behind to raise his son, losing all contact with them shortly thereafter.

Over the years, they both traveled separate, but similar paths; both cheering for the same teams, both with similar taste in music, both attending nursing school and both ending up working the same second shift on a state geriatric ward. The surprised siblings are reunited by their friend Issac, at an 1199 union rally in front of the state capitol building while they picketed over quality of care and cuts in health benefits for their institutionalized elderly clients. Their journey becomes a quest to get to know each other and make up for the long lost years.

Sabas Whittaker © 1997

AN INTERNATIONAL CONTROVERSY.

This is the story about fifty three men, woman and children led by a Joseph Cinque. His revolt against their capture in the Caribbean aboard the Spanish slave ship Amistad and the mutiny which resulted in a trial before the supreme court and brought former President John Quincy Adams out of retirement to defend the captive Africans against the federal government. This is the story of a fight for freedom and the embodiment of a struggle that began in 1839 and is still carried on and into classrooms, courtrooms, corporate halls and water fountains throughout our everyday lives in our fight for justice, equal rights and a piece of the pie.

(A stage drama with original music and dance movements, packed with original Afro Caribbean, Afro Latino, African American R&B, country rock and Reggae rhythms)

Sabas Whittaker © 1997

MODERN TIMES

Morris is reunited with longtime friend, Stephanie. Unknown to him several years back, Stephanie had fallen in love with him, but by now he was already married. He introduces her to his younger brother Martin, who marries her for her money.

Stephanie receives a large sum of money from an inheritance, but soon after receiving it, she contracts a terminal illness and dies. Martin, who had not been loyal to her and had treated her badly, soon after her death, he realizes that he was really in love with her. He becomes severely depressed and proceeds to drink himself to death and is unable to enjoy any of the money.

Sabas Whittaker ©1998

MUNDO MAYA

During an archeological expedition in Honduras, a young anthropologist realizes that he is actually a ré-incarnated Mayan prince. He turns to his newly acquired powers to prevent the growing pilferage of his ancestry's grave sites from foreign invaders and seeks to avenge and protect his country's archeological preservations. During such he recovers Noctezuma's stolen gold, which had been hidden in Honduras for over five hundred years.

Sabas Whittaker © 1997

TO SABAS

(by S. A. Brookter)

Astern man with a gentle way
I met him in September on a special day

He walked real proud to the podium stand
Was sure of himself yes a proud man
he read his poem with such feeling and style
I was deeply impressed in a short while

I looked at him and gave him a thumb's up sign
not realizing he'd become a good friend of mine
The day went on and it became my time to read
I read my poem and did it happily indeed

I heard a wolf whistle from whom I did not know
I laugh a bit and laugh out loud for it had tickle me so
The whistle had came from this gentle man
Yes the one who was special with a firm stand

We clicked right away I was truly impressed
I became comfortable and at my best
I'd felt to have find a true friend that day
I cannot wait to someday have him come my way

We dance we smiled shared laughter the day we met
it's an adventure which I'll never soon to forget

For I was happy with my new found friend
we both seemed to have relax on that special weekend
Thank you Sabas for having cross my path in D.C.
I hope to have impressed you as much as you did me.

WORDS OF ENCOURAGEMENT FROM MY FRIENDS, MY FANS AND MY CRITICS.

Sabas.

You filled your life with wonderful experiences that many people would only dream of having. Music was all that I had while growing up… I played the piano, marimba, and drums. As a child, music was my outlet. I can still remember how it feels to perform. The rush from feeling the music still fills my head. I wish that I had kept the music in my life, but every now and then I am able to incorporate my love for music into my poetry. You are an inspiration. Stay blessed. Veronica

Dear, Sabas.

I apologize if I seemed a bit impatient. I'm sure you were probably too busy to stop and talk to me. So thank you for taking time out to reply. You can reach me here or at xxxx@yahoo.com from this point on. I am doing okay except for the sinus infection am experiencing at the moment. I confer with the statement that you made in your poem *Spiritual Journey* that we sometimes have to experience the bad in order to appreciate the good. It seems like every guy I encounter these days are nothing but Nuckle Heads. I am starting to believe that in my former life or something I must have knocked off a family of five and their dog. And now I'm being punished to walk the earth the rest of my years as a single woman. If this is my fate, grant me one request. Please continue to send me the words from your soul, in them I will always find solace. Your poems are very spiritual and soothing to my soul. Lisa

Sabas

Who I am is pretty simple... I like simple things... quiet moments, the smell of rain, the feel of the wind , the sound of the ocean. And the harmonious sound of your voice as you read your poetry. Michelle

This is a lovely piece, my man ! I am really feeling the first lines.

Give your love

Don't await for assurance that they'll love you in return

Just sit and wait for it to grow in their hearts. Gus Romero

Hi Sabas, I received that beautiful poem, My African Queen, it was very strengthening; emotionally. I would love to have access to your site so I can read more of your work.   Thanks. Kimberly.

Sabas

That was beautiful! Who is she? Who inspired my friend to write such a lovely poem? I love it! I was impressed! When did you write this and how long did it take? The words are wonderful and appear to be so well thought out. Good Job! Can't wait for the book!!!!!!!! Siritha

That was absolutely BEAUTIFUL! I'm printing it out and putting in my bible for the future.

Thank you.

 Brenda

Hi, Sabas,

I want you to feel comfortable calling or saying hello any time you'd like. There's always room in my heart for people like you. I find you to be an absolute classic gentleman with good-old fashion values. I know you will continue to succeed in whatever you do... Can't wait to see your book in print, hold it into my hands and read it over and over . Thanks for being my friend...and for sharing your poems and screen plays. I'm not coming on to you I truly mean it in a very special way. You were the angel I needed to pull me out of the "rut" I placed myself in. I felt good about our brief conversation today. Thanks for being there. Thanks for helping to change my life with your literary gift. My mom told me to tell you hello!

Cheers,

Maria

Hi Sabas!

How was your vacation?

Just a short message to ask you how is your book coming along and how's the CD doing?

Keep in touch Thanks

Elman

Hello, Sabas.

I hope this message reaches you in blessed health. I'm new to all of this including this computer. I have been enjoying the work posted on your site Hats off to you. You are in my view a very talented poet. I am proud to even be considered to critique such unique and powerful writings.

Thanks for the opportunity

Mike

Hello Sabas..

Sometimes I am so busy that it does seem as if I am walking around in a dream state. There are moments when everything is just on automatic because I know that things have to get done regardless. Do you write poetry mainly to capture a moment in your life? Although what I write about isn't necessarily visible in my life. We all have desires and I guess this is my way of expressing the things that are important to me. I'm sure that is your advantage, huh? You still have that burning flame lite and that spiritual energy flowing keep it up. We're so proud of you.

Emmy.

Sabas:

I love this poem!!! I like the site. But the poem Earthly Eudimonia...beautiful!!!

Talk to you later! Ree

Hey,

Thank you for sending your web site. I've forwarded it to a couple of my friends who have an interest in the arts and writing. I'm going to continue to go to the site and read about all your projects before I fully comment, but I like is your mission statements, so I'll be writing you in the future about your site.

Thank you. Kadd

NICE!! Powerfully uplifting and moving! Keep it up!

Keva

What Matters Most Is How You See Yourself!

Nice work ! bro ! I want to be like you when I grow up!...LOL I see you have been gaining momentum over the years.

Brandon

Sabas the richness and style of this piece reminds me of one of my favorite poets TS Eliot. This was great!
Iron for rich ones,
they rust when they're old.
Oh poor gents thought,
they were buried in gold. V

Hello, Sabas!

It was nice meeting you. I am still trying to place your face with someone I met a few years ago. I was very impressed with your poems. I left there fully inspired... Great voice. I've heard your book will soon be out in print. Please keep me posted.

Thanks

Norma

Hi, Sabas!

I hope you are enjoying your well deserve vacation. I am back in Albany, the March paper is out and your poem is printed in it. Great feedback from the readers regarding your poem Tribute To A Homeless Vietnam Vet. I will be in New York City this weekend. I have two events to attend on Sunday. If you make it into the city please give me a call. I am already planning the April paper. It will be "career month." I have room and could use one of your spiritual poems Looking Back As I Move On. I hope you gotten yourself some R&R, though am sure the two things you wanted to get away from was your emails and phone. Without those is the only way you'd be able to get some rest.

Enjoy ! Tony

Hi Sabas!

It was great meeting and talking with you. It certainly sounds as if you are keeping busy.

As for the video shoot, I would love to be a part of that. Certainly, you would be welcome to use the barn. I'm flattered that you'd like to. As for dates perhaps next Saturday the 11th? If not, run some dates by me and we shall try to come to a mutually agreeable time. I think it is wonderful that you are moving on with your creative endeavors, and I wish you the best of luck with them.

Drop me a line or call me and we shall discuss plans.

My best to you...

Denise

Hi, Sabas. How are you.

I'd love to learn more about your music creations and travels and share some

of my record industry experiences and business adventures with you. Your poems are definitely moving.

Stay in touch

Andres